IGNITING
A PASSION
FOR READING

IGNITING A PASSION FOR READING

SUCCESSFUL STRATEGIES FOR BUILDING LIFETIME READERS

STEVEN L. LAYNE

FOREWORD BY GAIL BOUSHEY AND JOAN MOSER, "THE SISTERS"

STENHOUSE PUBLISHERS
PORTLAND, MAINE

Stenhouse Publishers
www.stenhouse.com

Credits
Front cover: Photos include *Guys Write for Guys Read*, © 2005 by Jon Scieszka; and *Zoe and Chloe on the Prowl*, © 2008 by Sue Limb, used by permission of the publisher, Viking Children's Books/Penguin Group.
Pages 56–57: Figures 4.1 and 4.2 adapted from *Children's Literature, Briefly*, 4th ed., by Michael O. Tunnell and James S. Jacobs. Copyright © 2008 Michael O. Tunnell and James S. Jacobs. Reprinted with permission.
Page 71: Figure 5.1 includes *Love the Baby*, text by Steven Layne, illustrations by Ard Hoyt; text © 2007 by Steven Layne, illustrations © 2007 by Ard Hoyt, used by permission of the publisher, Pelican Publishing Company, Inc.
Page 79: Figure 5.3 includes *Someday Is Not a Day of the Week*, text by Denise Brennan-Nelson, illustrations by Kevin O'Malley, text © 2005 by Denise Brennan-Nelson, illustrations © 2005 by Kevin O'Malley, used with permission from Sleeping Bear Press.
Back Cover: Photos include jacket design from *Some Dog!* by Mary Casanova, pictures by Ard Hoyt. Pictures copyright © 2007 Ard Hoyt. Reprinted by permission of Farrar, Straus and Groux, LLC.

Library of Congress Cataloging-in-Publication Data
Layne, Steven L.
   Igniting a passion for reading : successful strategies for building lifetime readers / Steven L. Layne ; foreword by Gail Boushey and Joan Moser.
      p. cm.
   Includes bibliographical references.
   ISBN 978-1-57110-385-7 (alk. paper)
   1. Reading—United States. I. Title.
   LB1050.L3819 2009
   372.41—dc22
                                                                                          2009029333

Cover and interior design by Blue Design (www.bluedes.com)

Manufactured in the United States of America

PRINTED ON 30% PCW
RECYCLED PAPER

15 14 13 12 11   9 8 7 6 5

To Dr. MaryEllen Vogt, for tapping shoulders . . . and changing lives.

CONTENTS

Foreword

After being invited to write the foreword for *Igniting a Passion for Reading,* and excitedly agreeing to do so, we suddenly remembered, "Hmmm, we've never written a foreword before." So, we looked at several models before deciding to try something different. Off we went to Starbucks, where we ended up taking a stroll down memory lane, starting with our first experiences with Steve Layne six years ago. Here is our conversation . . .

GAIL: It seems like yesterday that all the sixth graders at my school were reading Steve's novel, *This Side of Paradise.* It was everywhere I looked. I finally asked one of our sixth-grade teachers if I could borrow a copy. One of the kids saw it in my hand and said, "Mrs. B., are you going to read that book? Don't even start unless you have a lot of time, because you won't be able to put it down." I laughed, but she was right. I read it in one sitting, staying up way past my bedtime on a school night to finish it.

JOAN: Then you gave it to me, and I did the same thing! And I'll never forget truckin' through the exhibit hall at International Reading Association when you threw your arm across my chest, stopped me mid-stride, and hissed, "Joan . . . look. I think *Steve Layne* just walked by."

GAIL: We stalked him as he returned to his table, and I could barely breathe. Here was someone who could write a book that we'd both read in one sitting and that every sixth-grade boy and girl in the whole school devoured. We approached him, in the flesh, both gushing at once about the book. He must have thought we were completely nuts! He listened graciously, handed us his card, and said, "Well, I should come to your school."

JOAN: I remember we gave him one of our cards and, after walking away, snickered about what he would do with it. I said he'd probably use it to tidily dispose of chewed gum. Ha! It was only about a week later—when I was lying on the couch reading his book *Life's Literacy Lessons* during *American Idol* commercials—that the phone rang. The caller ID showed an area code I didn't recognize.

GAIL: A voice asked, "Is this one of 'The Sisters'?" You said, "Yes." He said, "Hi, Steve Layne calling." And you screamed! That's just embarrassing. It was like it was Oprah or something.

JOAN: Totally! After I screamed I said, "Steve Layne! I'm reading *Life's Literacy Lessons* RIGHT NOW!" He said he was planning a trip to Washington and remembered we were from there, and he wondered if we could set up a school visit. Our card didn't say we were in Washington. He remembered from our conversation at IRA.

GAIL: You called me right away, screaming, "You'll never guess who just called me!" After three wrong guesses I got annoyed and said, "Joan, just tell me!" When you said "Steve Layne," I couldn't believe it.

JOAN: So we set up the visit at your school—since your kids had been reading his book—and boy, did he teach us a lot about author visits! Planning school visits is one of the parts included in this book that we love so much.

GAIL: Man, is that the truth! His visits aren't a haphazard "Let's-have-an-author-come-in" assembly. Like the book says, a lot of thought and effort go into making an author visit successful. We distributed copies of his picture books to every classroom, and the teachers read them aloud prior to his visit. Steve even did an amazing presentation for our staff before school. Everyone left with renewed vigor for why we do this job and the importance of connecting kids with literature that engages their hearts and minds. Our friend Lori Sabo came over from her school and left with stars in her eyes, stating that she'd found her literacy soul mate.

JOAN: I'll never forget it. He had us laughing one minute and crying the next. Every time I hear the words "I thought of you," I think of Steve.

GAIL: Because of all the prep work, everyone felt they already knew him. The presentations Steve gave that day engaged every teacher and student. And the icing on the cake was when he left the manuscript for his book *Mergers* with our sixth graders, so they could read it first and provide feedback. Talk about authentic reading and writing—those kids were so motivated to read and to share their thinking!

JOAN: We spent so much time with him during that visit that our acquaintance began to blossom into genuine friendship. When it was time for him to go home, I felt the same way I used to feel when summer camp ended. People I'd known such a short time, but really loved and connected with, had to go back to their regular lives. I felt that same kind of grief, wondering if I'd ever see him again.

GAIL: Then we found out he was the keynote speaker at a conference where we were presenting in the fall. We were so excited to hear him speak, and boy, he did not disappoint. He took us to the mountains, renewed our joy and passion for teaching, pulled on our heartstrings, and gave us ideas we were determined to put into place on Monday morning.

JOAN: I was exhausted after listening to that speech! Afterward, we quickly hit the restroom, reapplied our makeup, and went to our first presenting session. To our horror, Steve walked in and quietly stood at the side of the room. We quit breathing momentarily and tried to ignore him. The last thing we wanted after hearing his five-star presentation before hundreds of people was to have him in our audience of fifty!

GAIL: That night, we met Steve for dinner at an incredible Thai place, and he offered some feedback on our session. He told us we were really onto something and encouraged us to get our message out there. "You have to write a book!" he said. Even though we'd already thought about writing a book more times than we could count, the goal and content were now being affirmed by someone we really respected. He shared with us the nuances of presenting well, explained how to give back to the community, and encouraged us to give thanks every day for the opportunity to participate in the lives of teachers and kids.

JOAN: The thing I'll never forget about that night was the look on his face when our darling waitress brought him a steaming hot bowl of pho. We later found out that our friend Steve was a stereotypical Midwestern meat-and-potatoes guy. I don't think he ate more than two tablespoons of the soup, with its transparent rice noodles bobbing and floating among pieces of tofu. Rumor has it he ordered a cheeseburger from room service when he got back to his hotel.

GAIL: That night he encouraged us to present at our first big-stage conference in Illinois. We were excited when the opportunity became real, and we were so warmly received by everyone there. We stayed in a beautiful historic hotel in downtown Springfield. To make things even more perfect, there was a Starbucks right across the street!

JOAN: Starbucks coffee usually brings good memories . . . but not this time.

GAIL: Some lovely teachers recognized us and wanted our picture, so I set my latte on the arm of a large, black, Edwardian-style chair. We turned around and took the picture. But when I turned back, my arm hit the cup, and the whole darn thing poured onto the beautiful white marble floor.

The hotel people were so lovely about it, quickly cleaning it up and assuring us that it wasn't a problem at all.

JOAN: I was mortified. But even worse than the Starbucks spill was that we didn't get to see Steve. He had to miss the conference after being stricken with Guillain-Barré syndrome. It was torture not being able to talk to him. We kept up with his condition and progress through the blog written by his wife, Debbie—thank goodness for her!

GAIL: Months later, the phone rang: "Gail, this is Steve." I was elated to hear his voice again. Then the joy turned to adrenaline-pumping trepidation when he said, "We had this really odd thing happen. The hotel has charged the Illinois Reading Council ten thousand dollars for coffee stains on their white marble floor. The tiles were imported from Italy. Your name is mentioned in connection with the stain, so I'm checking to see what you know about it." Seriously, my heart was in my throat. "Steve, the hotel cleaned it up . . . there was nothing there . . . they shouldn't charge you . . . it was okay, they assured us!" My mouth was blathering while my mind was thinking, "Oh no! Joan and I are going to have to pay for this!" I was still sweating and groveling when the gravity gave way, the tension melted, and he started to laugh—big, hearty, "gotcha" laughter. What a rat! Soon I had to get off the phone, since Joan and I were scheduled to teach a class that night. "Okay," he said. "But you *must* tell Joan the story—just the way I told it to you. Keep her going. Make her sweat."

JOAN: And that began the practical joke wars. We were out to get him! The following year we all attended a conference together, and Gail and I plotted our sweet revenge. Steve was tickled pink to introduce us at one of our sessions—that is, until Gail snuck up behind him while he was doing so and held up cue cards that read: **EVERYONE STAND; NOW EVERYONE SIT; NOW SAY "WE LOVE YOU, STEVE!"** And the audience members *did* it!

GAIL: The look on his face was priceless! It was *so* worth it. I'm always a little worried, though, about what his diabolical mind will come up with next.

JOAN: Our friendship reached a new level when he came to my school a few years later. We took him to Red Robin (having learned our lesson at the Thai restaurant), and we all traded cell phone numbers. Although we truly were friends by now, I still felt a bit starstruck. I had someone of celebrity status programmed in my phone—on *speed dial*, no less!

GAIL: Now we suspect that he only traded numbers with us so one of us could pick him up from the airport whenever he comes to town for business or pleasure!

JOAN: Seriously . . . remember when we were presenting in northern Canada, and the phone rang? "Joan, Steve here! I'm at SeaTac. Can you come get me?" "Steve! We aren't even in America!" The truth is, though, that no matter what we are doing, we usually clear the calendar when he calls. Any time spent with Steve is a gift. He's kind of like a brother to us now.

GAIL: So true! Okay, let's talk about the book. It really is amazing! It is a must-read for teachers and administrators of all levels about how to engage kids in reading and how to create a culture in schools that stirs a passion for books and authors.

JOAN: It will carry the message Steve's been delivering in person for years at schools and conferences to so many more people who haven't met him or heard his ideas yet. I love that my favorite stories from Steve's classroom are in there. Like the Jackson Miller story in Chapter 2— that's my all-time favorite.

GAIL: That might be my favorite too. It's in the section Steve includes at the end of every chapter called "In the Trenches." And isn't that what teachers really want to hear? The gritty truth from a real, live teacher in a real, live classroom? I love the candid honesty in the book; it made me feel like each chapter was a conversation he and I were having over coffee.

JOAN: You know, the other thing I love that makes the book so unique is the author reflection that opens each chapter. It was so fun to read about who inspired some of my favorite authors (Mem Fox, Karen Beaumont, Margaret Peterson Haddix, Sharon Draper, Neal Shusterman, and more). Steve even made me hope that, someday, one of my students will tell Oprah Winfrey and the entire world that I was the inspiration for his or her number-one best seller and career as a writer.

GAIL: This book makes you believe that could happen. I think teachers are going to love Chapter 10, where Steve organizes those strategies from the book that will inspire a love of reading into a quarterly schedule that all teachers can use, no matter what age they teach. In fact, I can see the strategies being used in any grade, K–12, and I really like the examples from multiple grade levels that he includes throughout.

JOAN: It just makes me sigh with happiness. The Steve you'll get to know in this book is the Steve we know and love. We believe he'll inspire you too with his characteristic truth, grace, humor, and heart. We truly can't wait to share him, our little brother, with you. No, wait. Let's make that our older—*way* older—brother, Steve Layne. We're honored and privileged to introduce you to *Igniting a Passion for Reading*.

—*Gail Boushey and Joan Moser, "The Sisters"*

Acknowledgments

We do not always *begin* writing out of heartfelt desire. Sometimes the dream is someone else's dream—of what we will write, of what we must write. And that is the case here. If this book brings about the change I dream of—for any school, any teacher, or any child—it will be because my editor, Bill "The Stalker" Varner, insisted that I write it. He spent a three-day conference in Alabama in 2003 following me around and thrusting his business card in my hand while I swatted it away time and again, telling him "I don't write those kinds of books." He followed up with e-mails and pursued by phone.

He's been in the audience again and again as I headlined conventions or spoke to small crowds. He shows up when I don't know he's coming, and, more important, he shows up when I ask him to be there. He lets me call him on weekends, at home, on his cell, at the office, and on Memorial Day weekend. He stood in my balcony when I couldn't speak, when I couldn't write, and when I couldn't move as Guillain-Barré syndrome paralyzed me for several months and nearly took my life in early 2005. He listens to my ideas. He had the guts to tell me that the first draft of Chapter 1 of this book read like a dissertation and to throw it away and start over. He helped me find my voice. He became my friend—and always will be.

We do not always *continue* writing out of great excitement for the product appearing before our eyes. Sometimes we are prodded by our competitive spirit to win a bet we made with an awesome friend. Rick Wormeli bet me a steak dinner plus dessert that he'd publish a young adult novel before I published a professional book, and I couldn't let him win because then he would laugh about it. When Rick laughs near me, the ground quakes because he is a California redwood, and I am Charlie Brown's Christmas tree. Now that I have won, he will not laugh. He will instead quietly pay for a very expensive dinner in a restaurant with no prices on the menu

. . . and I will laugh. Though the story of the bet is true, beyond that has been Rick's earnest encouragement for me to move this book forward. Losing the bet will truly make him happy; he knows how to celebrate the success of others. I have learned that it never hurts to have a California redwood in your corner.

We do not always *conclude* our writing in grand form, if at all. We may become weary near the end—our earlier enthusiasm hiding somewhere just out of reach. And then, in a sudden flash of inspiration, we think that maybe, just maybe, we can finish big after all—if an entire posse will ride to the rescue. My posse took the form of an incredible group of friends and exceedingly talented authors, including Mem Fox, Steven Kellogg, Joan Bauer, Candace Fleming, Eric Rohmann, Karen Beaumont, Sharon Draper, Neal Shusterman, Jordan Sonnenblick, and Margaret Peterson Haddix. Words cannot express the admiration I have for each of these talented authors and artists; their contributions to the book helped me maintain the momentum in the final hours. And finally, when I thought it couldn't possibly get any better, the Sisters—Gail Boushey and Joan Moser—who may actually be *my* sisters agreed to write the foreword to this book.

It is a given that tremendous appreciation goes to my incredible wife, Debbie, and our wonderful children, Grayson, Victoria, Jackson, and Candace, who allow me the time to write and remind me of the things more important than writing when such reminders are needed. My mother and extended family are consummate cheerleaders—always interested but never pressing me about the current project— and who could provide a finer second set of proofreading eyes than a retired teacher? Thanks, Aunt Sue! No one is blessed with a finer family.

I have to also grant a shout-out to many of my wonderful colleagues at Judson University, who care enough to understand my world and who know exactly what I mean when I say that.

Lastly, my thanks to the One who made the Heavens and the Earth, Who knew me before I was born, and Who has demonstrated His promises to me so tangibly in so many ways. Without the hope His love brings me each day, there would be no need for any of the rest.

ALITERACY POEM

Mrs. Thompson's second graders are amazing!

The principal says they can comprehend anything—

Even a medical textbook.

Mrs. Thompson's second graders are incredible!

The superintendent says their oral reading is completely seamless—

Like the gentle flow of an eternal spring.

Mrs. Thompson's second graders are fantastic!

The P.T.A. president says they finished the reading workbook *and*

the phonics workbook before the end of the Third Quarter.

Mrs. Thompson's second graders worry me.

You see, I'm the aide who works in Mrs. Thompson's classroom,

And I know something that the others don't.

Mrs. Thompson's second graders don't like to read.

(Layne 2001)

From *Life's Literacy Lessons: Poems for Teachers* by Steven L. Layne. Copyright 2001 by the International Reading Association. www.reading.org.

I wouldn't be the writer I am today were it not for my sensational high school English teacher, Miss Smith, who taught us rigorously—as if we'd learnt nothing at elementary school—all the nuances of grammar, spelling, and punctuation that we would need for the rest of our lives, as well as imbuing us with a mad passion for literature and a mania for words. No one writes well without a vast array of words to choose from: they're the colours in a writer's paint box, the notes on a writer's piano, the muscles in a writer's dancing feet.

Miss Smith read to us often, thereby providing me with hundreds of thousands of words. Sometimes she'd be reading a poem she loved so much she'd break down and say, "I'm sorry, girls. I can't go on! One of you will have to read instead." In later life I wondered if it was a ploy to get us to read complex texts without fear. Shakespeare and the great novelists and poets came alive on her tongue. The modulations of her voice created meaning for us where no meaning

would have been possible had we been reading silently on our own. There we were, in the early sixties, fifteen-year-old white girls in the middle of Africa, listening in awe to Shelley's "Ode to the West Wind," written in 1819, and loving it.

Knowing that learning is a by-product of getting things done, she made us write an enormous amount each week to put into practice the mechanics of writing we had learnt, and to put into personal use the fascinating words and ideas we had picked up from the literature we had read—and the literature that she had read to us. We were writing and learning as we were learning and writing: the mechanics of writing were inseparable from the act of writing. We loved her subject and we worshipped her.

—Mem Fox

The Missing Objective in the Teachers' Reading Lesson Plans: Igniting a Passion by Targeting Aliterate Readers

I t was early afternoon at Woodrow Wilson Elementary School, a building with attendance boundaries that include a women's substance abuse shelter, two homeless shelters, and a domestic violence shelter. A school with a mobility rate so high the principal told me that some teachers had, by May, an entirely different set of students than they had at the beginning of the year.

I had just finished giving an "author" talk to a group of very attentive fourth and fifth graders. As the students lined up with their teachers to exit the gym, Marie Boone made her way to where I was standing. I stared down into the earnest eyes of this precious child as she said, "What could someone do if they are only in fifth grade, but they know they want to write books? What advice could you give?" She then asked me, "What are the best colleges for someone who loves to read and wants to write books?"

Marie and I had a very mature conversation that afternoon. Her words spoke to me of her love affair with books and of the hope she found in reading. Despite what I later learned were tremendous hardships in her young life, it was evident to me that Marie was going places. Her experiences with books hinted at a way out. Marie had dreams; books had given her a vision for the future.

The brief opportunity I had to interact with the administration and staff at Marie's school made it clear to me that they were pulling out all the stops to give Marie and the other boys and girls a reason to dream. I knew that the administration viewed reading as a critical component for success because following the author talk they had me present a session for parents on promoting reading at home. At the end of the parent meeting, the school provided a free hardcover book for every child to take home. The way money is spent provides a window into our priorities, doesn't it? In the case of this particular school, the investment both financially and emotionally is in changing lives. They've come to the realization that books are one of the best tools at their disposal and that fostering a love of reading is their best chance to succeed. I applaud them.

A part of me was reluctant to leave Woodrow Wilson School that day. I wanted to join their mission right then and there! Practically speaking, I could not uproot my family and cancel other commitments to take a job in the school, but I sensed they understood the need to make the book-to-kid connection come alive and that had tremendous drawing power for me. On the flight home, I was burdened by my seeming inability to contribute in some way to these children. A solution came just as the wheels of the airplane hit the pavement.

When I arrived home, I drafted a letter to little Marie. I labored over the letter as if it were a graduate school thesis. Everything had to be perfect. I had done what I could for the larger group of parents and children with the time that I had, but Marie had come to me, specifically, looking for help. My letter gave her every reason to pursue her dream, every reason to believe it could happen. I gave her a "best book" list, and I told her that I believed in her. Then, I autographed some of my books to her and prepared them for shipping. I pulled the letter back out and added the P.S. "These books aren't a gift, Marie. We're *trading*. I'll be looking for a box of books you've authored arriving at my house someday in the future."

So goes fostering the love of reading in young people. Sometimes it's one child at a time, as in Marie's case. Other times we ignite the flame, a passion for books, in an entire roomful of young people all at once and then take all the right steps to keep it burning. For those educators who've lived it, there's no greater joy. My concern is that the teachers who *have* experienced this phenomenon are far too few in number, and that's the reason for this book.

Literacy skills have always been a precursor to success. Those who can read and write well become powerful communicators; such people are the movers and shakers of society in many cases. While this has always been true, today more than ever, strong literacy skills are a critical survival asset in a fast-paced, technological world (The Conference Board et al. 2006). More information is available today than at any time in history, and we have access to it more rapidly. Such advantages are meaningless, though, to those who cannot read or to those whose reading skills are so underdeveloped that comprehending a substantial or complex text structure is a seemingly insurmountable hurdle. In today's society, adults and schoolchildren whose reading abilities are deficient are treading water in a pool that has no shallow end.

It would seem that there is every reason to believe that school-age struggling readers are going to receive help—at least in the United States. Our federal, state, and local governments and agencies are enacting legislation left and right in an attempt to hold every person receiving a paycheck for working in public schools accountable for the students' success in reading. The focus on skills testing is unparalleled. It is also, in my opinion, unconscionable because it quietly propagates the idea that if we can identify weaknesses in skills and correct them, America's reading troubles will be abated.

Many educators categorize certain struggling readers as *disabled*—those whose skills do not allow them to comprehend text. They lack the ability; hence, the term dis*abled*. My concern, and the focus of this book, is for another population of readers who are not disabled per se—for they do have the ability to read. However, they are reluctant to become involved with books and/or the reading process in general. They are, in essence, dis*engaged* readers. Such students are too often forgotten by lawmakers, education pundits, and school boards, and the reason is simple: fostering a love of reading in kids is not a curricular objective. It's not tested by the state, it's not a component of any federal legislation, it's not in the district strategic plan, nor is it likely the focal point of any methodology courses at the local college or university. Despite the National Reading Panel's (2000) citing numerous studies that draw correlations between the amount of time children and young adults spend reading and their subsequent improvement in vocabulary development, fluency, and comprehension, we don't seem overly concerned with making reading an attractive choice for kids.

It would appear, then, that children don't need any help learning to love to read—it must just happen automatically. Right? Ask any practicing teacher if such automaticity is true for the majority of students these days and get ready for a very negative response. It's not necessarily that students *can't* read, it's that many of them *don't*. People, both children and adults, who have the ability but not the desire to read are termed *aliterates* (Mikulecky 1979), and they should be a source of concern for a nation that wants "no child left behind." The age-old concern of why Johnny can't read needs to change with the times. A new question, *Why won't Johnny read, even if he can?* needs some of our serious and undivided attention.

For most of my career, I have heard there is a keen desire to develop children as readers. It's been trumpeted by nearly everyone I've met who has any stake whatsoever in the educational process, yet I wonder if there exists among us even the most basic agreement on what a reader—a complete reader—really is. Figure 1.1 is a simple chart I created to visually explain to any listening audience what *I* mean when I call a child a reader. If I tell you that Bobby is a reader, you can bet that this kid has both the *skill* and the *will* to read. He can read, and he wants to. I don't worry so much about whether the left side of my circle is receiving appropriate attention with regard to personnel, funding, and instructional time, but I have grave concerns about the right side of the circle. When was the last time you had an inservice on issues related to teaching the *will* of reading? What exactly does that look like in first grade or in seventh? I spend nearly all my time answering that question to crowds of teachers for one simple reason: the affective component of reading education has not been a focus in most of their training.

If you believe, as I do, that reading is a choice and that it is not humanly possible to make anyone of any age read anything, then perhaps some time spent looking at how we can impact students in such a way that they will be more likely to make the choice to read deserves our attention. One of my favorite quotes of all time came from a classroom teacher who, all the way back in 1915, said:

> It should be the teacher's aim to give every child a love of reading, a hunger for it that will stay with him through all the years of his life. If a child has that he will acquire the mechanical part without difficulty. (Mayne 1915, 40)

FIGURE 1.1

A COMPLETE READER

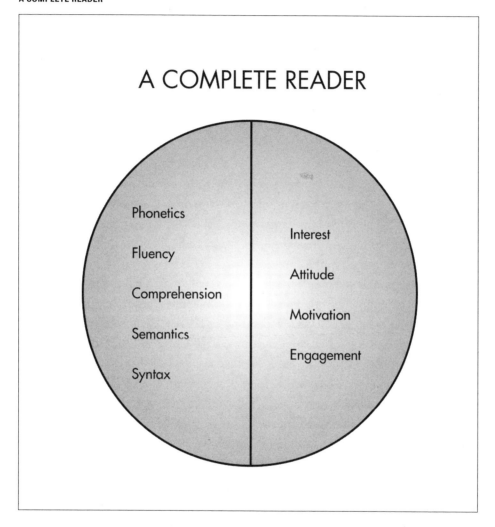

Now some will take issue with that last sentence, and I'm not going to argue the point that it may be oversimplifying things when it comes to certain learners. There are young people—I've taught them and so have you—who, even if they had a screaming desire to engage with books, would have tremendous difficulties to overcome. For Mayne to say "without difficulty" may be a stretch; however, I think the greater point is that the *will* could impact how much effort is put into the *skill*. In other words, if I want something badly enough, I'm going to work at it.

What I love the most about this quote is that it doesn't say it should be the "reading teacher's aim," or the "literacy coach's aim." The responsibility is not placed with the first-grade teacher, the language arts teacher, or the chair of the English department. This quote just says, "the teacher"—suggesting to me that we all could play a role. The question that excites me is, Who is willing? In an age where there seems to be a tremendous desire to institute change, especially based on what research is telling us, I am ever hopeful that people are going to finally be ready to listen to the types of issues addressed in this book.

I've never been able to figure out why more people can't see the contradiction between politicians, school board officials, and administrators who claim they want research-based initiatives and the corresponding exclusive focus on the left side of my circle—the skills. I'm all for teaching reading skills because without skills no one can read; however, if research is being given careful consideration, how are we missing the fact that our aliteracy rate has *surpassed* our illiteracy rate? This fact will be painfully obvious to anyone taking the time to carefully review data from *To Read or Not to Read* (2007), a noteworthy compilation put together by the National Endowment for the Arts. To sum up the multitude of data presented there, we have more readers who can read and don't than we do readers who can't read at all! Yet our focus as a nation remains almost exclusively on reading skills. The disconnect is frightening. Recent results from the Nation's Reading Report Card released by the National Center for Education Statistics (2008) show a gain of three points in the average reading ability of thirteen-year-olds. Now let's contrast this latest-and-greatest data on *ability* with the latest-and-greatest data on *use of the ability*, which reveals that less than one-third of thirteen-year-olds are daily readers (National Endowment for the Arts 2007, 7). I can think of no better way to make my point. What good is an ability you don't use?

The definition of best practice in education tends to swing back and forth in pendulum-like fashion, especially with regard to reading instruction. I say right from the start that I am not now, nor have I ever been, a "swinger" in terms of best practice in reading. I am not advocating that we retool the educational process and training of teachers and students to focus solely on the affective domain in reading, which incorporates such intangibles as attitude, desire, and motivation to read. What I am promoting is that those who care about education, especially those in positions of power and authority, acknowledge that, historically, we have given almost no attention to affective elements of reading instruction, and we are beginning to yield the terrifying results of that decision. If we continue to ignore the situation, I'm not convinced the future of our nation—controlled by the few people who do read—will be one governed by the people en masse, because people who don't read make all of their future decisions on what they *used* to know. How can they base their decisions on anything else? *Old knowledge* is all they have. As best-selling author Jim Trelease has said in his seminars, "Aliteracy is wicked. It's tearing this country apart . . . if you don't read much, you don't really know much. You're dangerous." His words remind me, eerily, of one of my undergraduate students, who wrote in his reading journal, "I get all of my information from television talk shows. Maybe I need to make some changes?" Maybe, indeed. I don't want such students representing the majority of the voting American public when I'm hanging out at the Heavenly Slumber Nursing Home and Medicaid is a hot topic in Congress! Our future leaders are sitting in our classrooms today. If they leave the schools as aliterates, who will suffer the consequences? I submit that, in the long run, we all will.

Historian Daniel Boorstin recognized the dangers of aliteracy back in 1984 when he was serving as the Librarian of Congress. He referred, in the landmark report *Books in Our Future* (Boorstin 1984), to the "twin menaces" of illiteracy and aliteracy, citing research statistics that only about half of all Americans read regularly every year. It would appear he knew what he was talking about, since 52 percent of Americans ages eighteen to twenty-four reported reading no books for pleasure in 2002, and that information evidenced a 12 percent decline from the 1992 study (National Endowment for the Arts 2007). Where will it be in 2012? I can hardly sleep at night when I think about it. And if you think it's just happening to readers when they get out of school, and then they "bounce back," think again. The percentage of Americans who read anything for pleasure in the twenty-five-to-thirty-four-year-old age group as well as in the thirty-five-to-forty-four-year-old age group experienced an 8 percent and an 11 percent decline, respectively, over this same time period (National Endowment for the Arts 2007, 7).

This is not some new phenomenon, either. In 1999, a Gallup Poll tracing the reading practices of Americans acknowledged that the number of Americans who don't read at all has been rising for the past two decades. In recent years, more has been written on the topic of aliteracy, including a high-profile article in the May 2001 issue of the *Washington Post* (Weeks 2001, C01), which amply supported the article's contention that "aliteracy is all around [us]" with multiple examples.

And where are America's schools in all of this? *Nowhere*, I'd say. In fact, the phrases *blind as a bat*, *head in the sand*, and *out of the loop* race to my mind when I consider the position of most school districts on aliteracy. Too many school leaders have never even heard the term. They're a long way from rallying their teachers to do anything about it.

I find it ironic that we live in a society that offers children and young adults so many more choices of what to do with their time than I had when I was their age, yet we fail to understand why so many indicators, including test scores, suggest that reading is on the decline. News flash: It's because most of the kids aren't in love with books—they're logged on or tuned in to some other form of entertainment and information. Research is all around us to substantiate this claim, including a report from the National Center for Education Statistics (1997), which states that reading attitudes deteriorate and voluntary reading drops as students progress through school. Big surprise. When we live in a society in which 43 percent of children ages four to six have televisions in their bedrooms (Kaiser Family Foundation 2003) and the average child watches twenty-eight hours of television a week (Trelease 2006/2007), what do we expect? Reading is no different than any other skill. What happens to a skill that isn't practiced? It atrophies. Conversely, a skill that is practiced grows stronger. Where are we headed if we don't start doing something more than running to the school library (if we even have one anymore—or ever did) for fifteen minutes and screaming, "Get a book! Hurry up! GET A BOOK!"? Linton Weeks (2001, C01) issued a warning when he wrote, "There may be untold collateral damage in a society that can read . . . and doesn't."

When I first began teaching (in the days when I understood reading instruction to summarily include teaching some skill lessons, reading a story excerpt, asking questions about the story excerpt, teaching more skill lessons, and then giving a test on the skills), I didn't have any students reading for their own enjoyment. My fifth graders were engaged in Game Boys, SegaGen, any number of television sitcoms, and *Silence of the Lambs*, but the bulk of them could identify a book only as something they'd seen on occasion. Are students today any different? Why read when you can go into a chat room and talk to "mystery friends"? Why read when you can get the information faster over the Internet? Why read when an increasing percentage of prime-time television shows and movies are being marketed to young people? Think about it. Why should kids soul-search through a copy of *The Giver* by Lois Lowry and discuss it with their friends when one of prime time's hottest teen dramas is offering a provocative episode showing a teenager going to bed with his schoolteacher? Do we really expect books to compete with this type of allure just because we have them sitting around the school on some shelves?

Enticing distractions aren't the only threat to reading, either. Consider the number of children being raised by single parents or living in a home where both parents are working full time. Although such situations are often necessary, the reality is that these parents come home from a full day of work and still have dinner to cook, carpooling duties for sports or other extracurricular activities, laundry, bills, and so on. They don't always have time to be reading role models in addition to all of their other responsibilities. As educators we can talk all we want about what parents can do to help us and what they should do to help us, but the reality is that we can only inform them. We cannot control them. Furthermore, in many homes the parents aren't the only ones whose time is spread too thin.

I remember vividly a parent conference I had a few years back. Mrs. Baker was distraught over Billy's lack of interest in books. Whatever could she do to help Billy learn to love books? I asked if she encouraged Billy's reading in any way—visits to bookstores or the library, reading a book together then watching the movie and comparing/contrasting the two mediums, reading and dialoguing about books together? No. There was no time for such things because Billy played on three soccer teams and one was a traveling team so he was often gone on weekends. Plus, he had private cello lessons, went to CCD, and was taking lessons in his father's native language at a special school once a week. While the story is tragically humorous, the fact that many kids are overscheduled must be acknowledged; as teachers we can only gently recommend to earnest parents that scaling back on activities may be necessary if they want their children to have time to read and experience great books.

And what about the kids themselves, who have the ability to read but are disengaged from books? Why *don't* they read? Some will say they don't have time, some will say there are no good books, and some will say they don't like reading. But I suggest that the real reason is that they have not been *taught* to value books. We have many kids leaving our schools without having truly experienced a book in an aesthetic and powerful way. We have students who have not known the thrill of victory that comes when careful reading and research has broadened their knowledge base, changed their thinking, or led to an exemplary paper or speech that informs others. We have kids who've yet to have a book inspire them to take action. We have young people who haven't *wondered* nearly enough . . . about anything! I'm talking about the kind of wide-eyed wonder that only a truly powerful story can evoke. Those who have encountered it know exactly what I'm talking about, but I fear that many students have yet to experience what I'm describing. Until they do, they will not value the experience of reading.

The traditional curriculum places little to no emphasis on the value of reading from an aesthetic perspective. There is considerable talk about how important reading is, and we are very committed to making sure everyone can read, but when it comes to the actual physical act of imparting the value of reading books to students, we are not as adept as we need to be. Why? The likely reason is that the affective domain of reading has always been the neglected stepchild, both in theory and in practice. Attitude, motivation, and other such intangibles don't lend themselves to finely tuned, measurable, empirical studies and concrete theoretical models, so they tend to be avoided lest they solicit volumes of skeptical remarks from the learned. When it comes to the aesthetics of reading, we can't give a *test* to see how we are doing or *if* what we are doing is impacting the students. We do not see significant time and money devoted to teaching the value of books, fostering the love of reading, and building the motivation to read in young people. Such goals are not easily measured nor are they measurable beyond question; hence, they have not found their way into the traditional school curriculum, which remains rooted in an exclusive focus on the mechanics of reading.

Meanwhile, a larger and larger percentage of students haven't had enough positive experiences with literature in school to foster a desire to spend any time with books. Many don't describe themselves as readers at all, let alone consider themselves readers for life. *We* have failed to convince them that they are readers. We may have taught them the skills, but without the desire to use those skills, where is the benefit? In many cases, it will be what happens or doesn't happen in school that is going to make the difference. My friend Kelly Gallagher couldn't be more on target with his contention that "Today, more than ever, valuable classroom time presents the best opportunity—often the only opportunity—to turn kids on to reading" (Gallagher 2009, 2).

I ask those who are truly concerned about reading instruction to become my partners in igniting a passion for reading in schools. I ask you to raise your voices in faculty meetings and college classrooms, in literacy conferences and at parent nights, and educate people about aliteracy—the "invisible liquid seeping through our culture" (Weeks 2001, C01).

And then . . . offer your listeners hope, ideas, and solutions for change. That is what the rest of this book is about—the *hope* that the situation can change and that practical classroom-based solutions will turn the aliteracy tide. After all, we're teachers. We're in the hope business. So, from my classroom to yours, I'm going to give you the very best I have to help *you* help the kids. And, perhaps, you'll then tell someone else. Together, let's write (in ink) a *new* objective in our Reading Lesson Plan Book: fostering a lifetime love of reading in our students.

Words tell stories. And words themselves *have* stories.

That wasn't something I understood until I was a high school freshman sitting in Marie Fetters's college prep English class. Until then, I mostly took words for granted. But Mrs. Fetters gave us daily word derivations—imparted in a way that made the whole class feel like we were hearing juicy gossip. It's been almost thirty years since I took that class, but I still remember many of the tales: *Tawdry* entered the English language because the nuns at St. Audrey's weren't very good at making lace. *Bedlam* became a word because there was an insane asylum at Bethlehem, England. In both cases, the words evolved and changed as the language evolved and changed and people needed new meanings.

Since then, I've witnessed the evolution of English for myself: In the 1980s, Michael Jackson made *bad* mean good. My kids tell me that *sick* now means the same thing as *sweet*.

My own daughter, as a high school sophomore, took an etymology course. She had a great teacher, but she also had enormous word lists intended mostly to help with test scores. I don't remember Mrs. Fetters's ever uttering the words, "This will help you on the SAT." She made it clear that she was teaching us about words just so we could understand our own language—so we could share her awe at the crazy glory that is English. Over the years, I was blessed with lots of great teachers who guided me toward loving books and becoming a writer. But I'm particularly grateful to Mrs. Fetters for teaching me to value the words themselves.

—Margaret Peterson Haddix

Coaches Who Know Their Players Win More Games: Igniting a Passion by Knowing Your Students

I t has to be true, right? I mean, there are some things we should not have to spend our time looking up statistics on because they just make sense. Though I knew my impromptu research would be lacking both validity and reliability in the empirical sense, I checked out my hypothesis with my brother-in-law Tory, who coached our Judson University Women's Basketball Team to five NAIA (National Association of Intercollegiate Athletics) National Tournaments within a nine-year period. When I asked him if my chapter title rang true, his response as a former championship coach was, "most definitely. It makes all the difference." And it does. It makes all the difference on the court, and it makes all the difference in our schools.

It's often said that the three most important words people need to hear are "I love you." I would never argue with that. But I'll tell you the *four* most important words that I think kids—our own and our students—need to hear. They are "I thought of you." Those words, supported with tangible evidence, can work miracles in the life of a disengaged reader.

Several years ago I found myself in one of my least favorite places—an end-of-the-year teacher meeting where the current teacher tells you about all the kids you're going to have next year. Now don't get me wrong, I want to know if a student has vision problems, is deathly allergic to peanut butter, or has just moved here from Bulgaria and can't speak a lick of English. I did not, however, need for Helen to tell me that "Danny will be a real pain next year. And he hates reading, by the way—everything about it.

Won't read at all. He can—just won't."

"Well, Helen," I said with all the charm I could muster, "what is Danny interested in?"

"Nothing."

I squelched my desire to begin coloring on Helen's face with a turquoise Sharpie that was temptingly within my reach. "Why, Helen, everyone is interested in something. Did you ever ask him about his interests?" I queried.

"No time for that. Too much to do," she said and proceeded to march on down her list like a sniper at a shooting range. Helen retired recently; I didn't make the party.

Of course, Danny *was* interested in something: motorcycles. And when I showed up with magazines about motorcycles, nonfiction books about motorcycles, and *The Mouse and the Motorcycle* by Beverly Cleary, I was extending an olive branch to a boy who'd spent an entire year of school thinking there was nothing he would like to read. "Daniel, sir," I said in my best official voice, "When I saw all these motorcycle books and magazines, *I thought of you*. Would you like to look at them?" With wide-eyed wonder, Danny took the whole stack, found himself a cozy spot, and went to work. (I thought to drag Helen down the hallway by her hair and make her look at him reading but decided against it. She's bigger than I am.) Danny checked out two books from the library and "borrowed" my magazines for many weeks; moreover, a relationship was cemented between us that day. When I said, "I thought of you" and handed him those books and magazines, there was no denying that I had indeed spent time just on him. He knew it, and it was a tremendously important first step. One that we both needed to take.

Interest Inventories

The question I hope you're asking just now is, How did I *know* that Danny liked motorcycles? If you weren't already asking that question, stop here for a moment and ask it before proceeding. (See there, I'm setting a purpose for your reading.) I knew about the motorcycles because I had given my students an interest inventory on the first day of school to find out a little bit about each one of them. I'm all about working smarter—not harder—and I have found that these interest inventories give me the information I need while taking only a few minutes of instructional time to administer. I generally choose from two types of inventory. The first type offers choices and categories from which the students can select. Figure 2.1 (see Appendix D for a blank version) can be used with very young children. I recommend putting a copy on each student's desk and another on the overhead projector for you to use as a guide, reading aloud each possibility and helping the students understand how to check off topics they especially like. Figures 2.2 and 2.3 (see Appendix D for blank versions) begin with checklists followed by some simple fill-in-the-blank opportunities and then some genre preferences to circle at the bottom. These samples come from third grade (a shout-out to one of my graduate students, Theresa Tuttle, for her contributions to this third-grade sample) and seventh grade, but provide ample opportunities for adjustment by teachers at various grade levels. Feel free to copy them, alter them, and so forth. Every strategy and idea in this book has to become yours if you're going to use it, so don't feel like anything is sacred.

The second type of interest inventory (Figure 2.4; see Appendix D for a blank version) is a series of questions that the kids will think is basically unrelated to books; however, every single question *is* actually related to books (I love it when we're sneaky!). For example, question 9 asks, "If you had the chance to meet any famous person, living or dead, who would it be?" Well, the answer to that question gives me information to go searching for just the right biography or autobiography! Get the picture? If you do, you might be sneaky, too. Obviously, the number and type of questions can be easily altered to target specific grade levels without difficulty.

Let's get practical now. Let's say I give these interest inventories on the first day of school to ninety kids. What do I *do* with all these papers next? I put them in a file folder, and over the next few weeks, I simply begin to observe which kids are the most disenfranchised when it comes to books. These kids become my *targets*. Sssshhhh! Obviously, all ninety kids don't need my help, and even if they did, I couldn't get to them all. But I do try to select those who need help the most, then head to the incredible, amazing school librarian, and we start to do our thing—pulling books, finding, hunting, searching for any type of print that matches a given student's "targeted" interest. We try to hit at least two kids each quarter, but sometimes we can do more. And all we do is simply build the biggest pile of reading materials we can find on subjects of interest to our *targeted student*, then we pull him or her aside and deliver the message in both word and deed: *I (We) thought of you.*

FIGURE 2.1

WHAT DO YOU LIKE? INVENTORY

What Do You Like?

Name _Alex_

Put an "X" by the things you like.

X	animals	___	trains
___	tools	___	circus
___	dancing	___	jokes
X	books	X	bugs
X	sports	X	cooking
X	games	___	computers
X	music	X	art

FIGURE 2.2 SIDE A

READING AND ME INVENTORY

Reading and Me

Name _Ayleen_

1. How well do you think you read?

☺ 😐 ☹

2. How do you feel about reading at home?

☺ 😐 ☹

3. How do you feel about reading at school?

☺ 😐 ☹

4. Do you have books at home that you read?

(Yes)   No

5. What are your favorite t.v. shows?

Hannah Montana, Wizards of Waverly Place, iCarly, The
Suit life on deck, The Suit life of Zack and Cody.

6. What is the best movie(s) you have seen?

Beverly Hills Chihuahua, and Another Cinderella
Story.

7. If an author could write a book just for you, what would it be about?

It would be about a girl who's dog
died and she was crying real hard.

FIGURE 2.2 SIDE B

READING AND ME INVENTORY

Circle what you like to read:

comic books	magazines	newspapers
non-fiction books	poetry	plays
(mysteries)	(funny books)	adventure books
("how to" books)	books about the past	

Circle what you like to read about or what you want to learn more about:

(famous people)	music	other countries
insects	(dancing)	sports
aliens	monsters	(jokes)
(poetry)	solar system	(friends)
(animals)	planes	cars
(cooking)	making crafts	drawing

Other _____

FIGURE 2.3

INTEREST INVENTORY

Interest Inventory

Name _Alexa_

Place a check beside anything on the list below that you would like to know more about.

___ auto mechanics	___ construction	X electronics
___ famous people	___ woodwork	___ history
___ motion pictures	___ foreign lands	___ printing
___ electricity	X art	___ circus
X music	X monsters	X poetry
___ theatre	X computers	X animals
___ insects	___ science	___ cars
X dancing	___ singers	___ planes
___ geography	___ detectives	X outer space
X cooking	X jokes	___ radio
X sports	___ writing	___ trains

If an author wrote a book just for you, what would it be about? _a realistic story about something that could possibly happen._

If _my friend_ recommended a book to me, I would probably read it.

Circle what you like to read.

comic books	animal stories	magazines	science fiction
mysteries	humorous books	newspapers	historical fiction
romances	biographies	plays	adventure stories
poetry	short stories	fantasies	"how to books"

FIGURE 2.4

INTEREST INVENTORY

Name _Lauren_

Interest Inventory

1. What do you like to do in your spare time? Swim/diving, listen to music, computer, bake, and sports.

2. Do you belong to any clubs or organizations? If so, what are they?
   no

3. What kind of movies do you like?
   Comedies

4. Do you have any favorite sports?
   volleyball, basketball, and gymnastics

5. If you had three wishes, what would they be?
   to become a teacher, no more wars, and 3 more wishes.

6. What kind of books do you own?
   mysteries

7. If you had a surprise day off from school, how would you spend it?
   Sleep in, hang out with friends, and go to the mall

8. If you could transport yourself to any time or place in the past, where would you go?
   Sometime in the future

9. If you had the chance to meet any famous person, living or dead, who would it be?
   Taylor Swift

10. If you could pick any three books from a bookstore for free, what might they be about?
    mysteries, humor, adventure

11. If you could go on a trip to any place in the world today, where would you go?
    Paris

I'm not saying it works perfectly every time. I won't make the claim that every kid will read everything you select. I can't promise that your librarian will help or that he or she will be amazing and incredible like mine have always been (though most school librarians are indeed both amazing and incredible). And goodness knows, you probably can't find a way to do this for every single kid who might need it. But . . . I've always looked at it this way: I may not reach everybody, but every time I reach somebody, I'm doing more than I would be doing if I were doing nothing. It's one more thing to try, and it surely can't do any harm.

Student Self-Assessments

As well as interest inventories, I like to see students take some kind of initial self-assessment right at the beginning of the year. Again, it's no great loss of instructional time, since students can complete them in just a few minutes, but the information gained is critical. As it is with skills, so should it be with elements of the affective domain—reading interest, attitude, motivation, and engagement need a benchmark. We have to know where kids are in the beginning if we're going to monitor progress. I have often used an Initial Self-Assessment (Figure 2.5; also in Appendix D) to get a handle on where my students are at the beginning of the year. I ask them to respond honestly and am clear that there is no penalty for any type of answer. "For example," I say to them, "Number 6 asks you to identify the best book you've ever read. If you feel you've never read a book that was good, you may absolutely write 'none.' All I want is honesty, guys."

Obviously, perusing these in the opening week of school gives me an important sense of who my students are as readers. If I don't know anything about them as readers, it would seem there would be little chance that I would be able to entice them to read anything—because remember, it's their choice whether they read. I can't make them do it, and neither can you.

At the end of the school year, I will give them a Final Self-Assessment (Figure 2.6; also in Appendix D) that is going to be very similar to the original one they took when we began our year together. There are differences between the initial and the final self-assessment, but they are subtle. Take a few moments to compare them. As you discover the differences, ask yourself *why* you think I made the changes I did. What was I looking for?

FIGURE 2.5

INITIAL SELF-ASSESSMENT—READING

Name _____

1. I enjoy reading the following types of print:

   ☐ books   ☐ magazines   ☐ newspapers

   ☐ poems   ☐ short stories   ☐ plays

2. I choose to read books that are not assigned in school . . .

   ☐ often   ☐ sometimes   ☐ never

3. My attitude about reading is . . .

   ☐ positive   ☐ neutral   ☐ negative

4. I like to read books from the following genres:

   ☐ nonfiction—informational   ☐ historical fiction   ☐ science fiction

   ☐ traditional fantasy   ☐ modern fantasy—low   ☐ modern fantasy—high

   ☐ nonfiction—biography   ☐ nonfiction—autobiography ☐ realistic fiction—mystery

   ☐ realistic fiction—adventure ☐ realistic fiction—humor ☐ realistic fiction—classics

5. When I compare books that I have really enjoyed, some things they all have in common are _____

   _____ .

6. The best book I've ever read is _____

   _____ .

7. Some of my favorite authors are _____

   _____ .

8. I could improve my reading skills if _____

   _____ .

9. People whose book recommendations I value include _____

   _____ .

10. I could make more time for recreational reading if _____

    _____ .

11. A reading goal that I would like to achieve for this school year is _____

    _____ .

FIGURE 2.6 SIDE A

FINAL SELF-ASSESSMENT—READING

Name _____

1. I enjoy reading the following types of print:

   ☐ books   ☐ magazines   ☐ newspapers

   ☐ poems   ☐ short stories   ☐ plays

2. I choose to read books that are not assigned in school . . .

   ☐ often   ☐ sometimes   ☐ never

3. My attitude about reading is . . .

   ☐ positive   ☐ neutral   ☐ negative

4. I like to read books from the following genres:

   ☐ nonfiction—informational   ☐ historical fiction   ☐ science fiction

   ☐ traditional fantasy   ☐ modern fantasy—low   ☐ modern fantasy—high

   ☐ nonfiction—biography   ☐ nonfiction—autobiography   ☐ realistic fiction—mystery

   ☐ realistic fiction—adventure   ☐ realistic fiction—humor   ☐ realistic fiction classics

5. I have grown this year as a reader because _____

   _____ .

6. The reading selection that I liked the most this year was titled _____

   _____ .

7. I liked this selection because _____

   _____ .

8. The reading selection that I liked the least this year was titled _____

   _____ .

9. I did not enjoy this selection because _____

   _____ .

10. A book I enjoyed that was recommended to me this year was titled _____

    _____ .

11. Some of my favorite authors are _____

    _____ .

FIGURE 2.6 SIDE B

12. This year, my reading skills have . . .

☐ improved a lot ☐ improved a little ☐ stayed the same

13. This year my recreational reading habits have . . .

☐ improved ☐ stayed the same ☐ declined

14. People whose book recommendations I value include _____

_____ .

15. A reading goal that I would like to achieve for next school year is_____

_____ .

I've always made a habit of running the Initial Self-Assessment on green paper and the Final on pink. Green was for "go" the beginning of the year, pink (we could never seem to afford red paper) for "stop" at year's end. Of course, the kids rarely ever remember by the end of the year that they filled these out on day one. In fact, I have never had a student say anything like, "Hey, didn't we do these on the first day of school?" Of course, if one of them did, I would simply respond with the trademark wit that helped me survive with middle school students for so many years, "Yes," I would reply with an overdone smile. "And now here you find yourself doing it again."

The great fun comes when, in the final week of school, my students complete this Final Self-Assessment, and I magically pull out the Initial Self-Assessment from the beginning of the year. I wait until I am certain every student is completely done with the final assessment. What happens next is *very* metacognitive. It could be described with a whole bunch of highly impressive multisyllabic words that I don't want to use because then you won't like this book, so we'll just say it's "way good."

I say to my students, "Ladies and Gentlemen, you are looking at what is likely to be a very true and honest reflection of who you were as a reader on day one of this school year and who you are as a reader today. Our data come from a highly reliable source—you." I then invite them to truly study the data, compare and contrast their responses, and make random notes of their observations regarding *change*.

What comes next is a writing assignment that will be done during class time.

It will *not* be graded *unless* they want to trade this finished piece out for one that received a less-than-favorable mark during this final quarter. They must make that decision, of course, in advance of my grading it. In other words, I don't grade it unless they feel so good about it when they are done writing that they say something like, "Grade this piece of writing and exchange it for the grade I earned on the personification paper where I pretended I was a Kleenex full of snot."

I strongly advise you, readers, to offer up my "trade the grade" option because some of the best pieces of writing your students will ever produce may be demonstrated in this assignment. For the actual writing, I allow approximately 120 minutes of class time. Some students get so into it that they choose to work on their papers at home as well. The paper must focus on how they have changed as readers—or how they have not. Titles are optional; sometimes they can be very creative, so allowing the option of a title is a good idea.

I encourage students to explore in detail answers to some specific questions (see the list that follows) in their "changed reader" papers. It is important to let them know that, although at first glance many of these questions can be answered with a word, the purpose in my presenting them is so students can use them to launch points for solid and interesting written responses. I also suggest that if there has been more than one change, they write about all of them and that they may be creative in the way they structure their papers.

QUESTIONS TO EXPLORE IN A "CHANGED READER" PAPER

In what areas of your reading have you noticed a change?

Has anyone else noticed a change?

How fast did the change happen?

Did you notice or think about the change happening before it became evident in your survey comparison today?

How dramatic or significant is/are the/these change(s)?

Why do you think the change occurred? Would the change have occurred all by itself?

How do you feel about this change in your reading behavior?

Would you have predicted this change was going to happen this year?

What will be necessary to keep you moving forward and growing as a reader?

In all my years of offering this opportunity to my readers, I have never had a student say there has been no change. If you, your team, or your school breathes life into the program I am endorsing in this book, I have a strong feeling that you'll see similar results. And best of all, these are our own kids telling us, in effect, that what we've done has mattered. That it's made a difference. That they are different readers when they leave us than they were when they arrived. I don't know about you, but that's why I became a teacher in the first place.

Goal Setting

I will never, *ever*, forget the difficulty I had in one of my schools at the annual faculty meeting, during which the principal always announced to the teaching staff the goals that had been set *for us* by the board of education for the upcoming year. Good friends would harness me to my chair and duct-tape my mouth shut at this yearly meeting, for fear I would start a revolution and get myself and multiple other people fired for insubordination. I'm sorry, but is this not the most ridiculous thing you have *ever* heard? How motivated are you to reach goals *someone else* is setting for you—and especially an entity you do not even believe should exist? (But that's for the book I'm still threatening to write.) I never cared two hoots about their goals. I might have, if I'd been a part of the process of crafting them, but I wasn't. Apparently, my input regarding the goals that my daily work would either achieve or fail to achieve for our district was not viewed as a significant factor in their plan for goal creation. Is it any wonder that so many of our schools are in such a mess? One of my best friends and colleagues would regularly repeat this sentence in our weekly team meeting: "The system is flawed." I believe she may have made a seriously important discovery.

I believe that goal setting can be tremendously motivating—when the people setting the goals are the same people who will be working to make them successful. We can use goal setting to build rapport with kids that will energize and excite them—creating a kind of "catch the wave" mentality. I have found that goal setting works if we set goals for ourselves right along with our students, if we keep the goals visible and refer to them often, and if we show the kids we really do care about how they are progressing by talking with them about their goals one-on-one.

Some of you may reach for the oxygen mask when you read about one-on-one discussions, and I don't blame you. If you've walked that road of "I'm going to conference individually with every child on his or her work every week," and then not been able to do it and felt like the biggest loser ever, you're not alone: been there, done that. But stick with me because I'm going to talk about a way to manage goal setting and conferencing that will not lead you to run screaming into traffic.

The first thing I like to do with my students is to brainstorm different kinds of reading goals. We fill the whiteboard, chalkboard, overhead transparency, chart paper, or whatever surface we're using with as many kinds of reading goals as we can identify. Examples include reading from a new genre, reading multiple works by the same author, reading for a certain number of minutes or hours weekly, reading a certain number of books for the quarter, and reading books recommended by a specific person. Of course, the students often come up with many more, but this gives you some idea of what types of goals we often create. I also model for them my own goal for the upcoming quarter, which tends to be a great motivator. When they see that I feel I have room to grow as a reader, they feel a little less like lab rats going through the motions for the teacher.

In the second quarter of my first year teaching sixth grade, my goal was to read three historical novels—all by James Lincoln and Christopher Collier but from different periods of history. I explained to my students that I not only had loved the novel *My Brother Sam Is Dead* when I first read it but that I also had been amazed at how much I learned about history. I extolled the virtues of these authors, who are brothers, and jumped up and down over the fact that one is actually a history professor. "So I can be even more confident I'm getting the good stuff!" I told them. I also admitted that my tendency is to read more on the American Revolution because I love that period of history and know so much about it. Thus, my goal was to stretch myself by allowing only one of the three books I would be reading to be set during that time period. Figure 2.7 (see Appendix D for a blank version) shows my goal sheet; I give the same sheets to the kids.

Once we've brainstormed goals and I have modeled my quarterly goal, I ask my students to set a strong reading goal for the upcoming quarter: one they feel is attainable but will also push them a bit. We discuss how unrealistic goals may quickly lead us to feel that we've failed while goals requiring little effort don't yield much satisfaction. I give my students about fifteen minutes at the end of class to get started and tell them that tomorrow, I will ask each of them to tell me about their goal and give me a copy of a written commitment to work toward it.

The next day, when the students come into the classroom, a giant "you couldn't miss it if you tried" copy of *my* reading goal commitment for the quarter is posted at the front of the room to remind them that we are in this together.

I let the kids turn their goals in to me and then give them some free reading time or a break of some kind (see Chapter 8) while I wander the room with a class list in hand. I have each student look me in the eye and verbally tell me his or her goal. I note the goal in my own version of shorthand on my class list. If Susie says her goal is to read two historical fiction novels this quarter because that is a genre she typically avoids, I will congratulate her on stretching herself, suggest any historical fiction titles I know that are likely to grab her, recommend she ask the librarian to pull some of the best of the genre for her to preview, and write "2 hf" next to her name on the class list (my shorthand for "two historical fiction books"). I can generally get through a class of twenty-five students in about thirty minutes.

Next, I photocopy my list so that I have one copy at the front of my classroom and one at my desk in the back. The idea is that there's always a copy handy. Now, that I have looked each of my students in the eye and heard about his or her goals, I set to work reminding them that these goals really matter, and that I care about their efforts to succeed.

Over the quarter, I use the passing period as kids are coming into the room and random spare moments when kids are working at their seats on an assignment to check in on how they are coming along with these goals. Sometimes I can only get to one student in a day, but other times I may get to five. I don't hold myself to a number, but I always have my class list with my shorthand on it so that I can say, "Susie, how's it going on that historical fiction goal?" I name her goal, and I inquire with interest. It's a conversation, not an inquisition. I make sure to talk about how I'm doing on my goal if she fails to ask. I put a check by her name. Once I've touched base with everyone in the class, I simply start over with a different-color pen for the second set of check marks. It is *amazing* how much more interested and excited

FIGURE 2.7

DR. LAYNE'S READING GOAL FOR SECOND QUARTER

NAME _Dr. L_

Reading Goal for _2nd_ Quarter

A strong reading goal will

- Stretch you in some new way
- Motivate and interest you
- Be reasonable

My goal this quarter is _to read three historical novels by the Collier brothers. Each novel will be set in a different period of history._

This is a strong goal for me because _I tend to choose HF set during the Revolutionary War. I need to build background knowledge about other times in history._

students are when they realize these goals are not just another "teacher thing" that is going to be forgotten two weeks later.

About halfway through the quarter, we take some time one day to break into groups and give a goal update. What was the goal? How am I doing? Was it too ambitious? Too easy? What about next time? I start the conversation by giving my own goal update to the whole class. Sometimes, the session evolves into a whole-group time of letting anyone who wants to give an update for the whole class. I love the sense of team spirit that is engendered; these goals are something we are all doing together. Again, I won't say every student loves it or gives it 100 percent effort because that's rarely true of anything we try. But I will say that I have found any effort we make to know our students better, any visible attempt we demonstrate to take an active interest in them will yield more cooperation, more motivation, and more determination for them to grow themselves as readers.

FROM THE TRENCHES

Perhaps my greatest success story in building a reading bridge by means of tapping a student's interest and making use of solid rapport came from my experiences with Jackson Miller. At some point in your career, you will be the favorite teacher of one of your students—and you will know it. Jackson gave that honor to me when I was his sixth-grade teacher. We had a great relationship, but I never really succeeded in building in him any intrinsic interest in books. If he read, it was to please me. Seventh grade rolled around, and we were together again. I received a call requesting a parent conference very early in the year. I had never met Jackson's parents but was happy to oblige.

On a night that lives in infamy (with me at least) Jackson's parents arrived with him in tow, and the father went from a mild-mannered Clark Kent-type to Supernut faster than a speeding bullet. He whipped a chair across my classroom and began berating his son with very hurtful words because the boy was not a straight-A student. Mother then chimed in that she thought her husband was nuts because how could a boy like Jackson get straight As when he had no real abilities to speak of? The two of them bantered about like this for quite some time, and Jackson did his best to fight back the tears that slowly began to leak from his eyes. He was humiliated, and my presence, my hearing what was clearly a secret he kept to himself (that his parents were raving lunatics) made things just that much worse in his mind, I'm sure.

I made no headway with his parents and left school that evening feeling like a real loser. I don't know what you do when you get stressed. Some people drive fast, some people eat chocolate, some people drink liquor. I buy books! I drove straight to Barnes and Noble, and I just started buying. Of course, Jackson was on my mind the entire time, and I remembered that he was particularly fond of Navy SEALs. I had taught many boys over the years who were into Navy SEALs—Jackson did not stand out in that sense—but whatever the reason that was the only thing that popped into my mind as I coasted over to the kids' section and found a bin labeled "animal books."

I began to sift through the titles somewhat hurriedly. (I must now pause and ask that you not allow the chain of events that follows to reflect poorly on Northern Illinois University—the institution that awarded me my doctoral degree.) A clerk walked up and asked if I needed help. I replied, "I don't think you can help me because you're all out of Navy seal books. I've found books on different kinds of elephants—Asian and African—and different kind of giraffes—reticulated and Rothschild—but all you have on seals are just regular seal books. They don't even mention Navy seals in the index. See, here?"

She took a step back rather quickly and looked me up and down. She then spoke these words: "You're serious, aren't you?"

"Young woman," I replied in a bit of a put-out tone, "I am quite serious. There is not one mention of Navy seals in any of these books. Not *even* in the book titled *Seals!*"

It is too painful to continue. Let us just say that I became more educated about all things military and left the bookstore that evening with some Navy SEAL books. When I presented them to Jackson in private the next day, he looked at me curiously—as if waiting for an explanation of why he warranted special treatment from the teacher. I could not say to him that, for me, it was either this or I would have to hire a hit man to take out his parents, so I said, "It was Navy SEAL night at the bookstore last night—and of course I *thought of you.* Jackson's eyes misted over, and he looked me in the eye and said, "I'll read every word." And he did.

Several weeks later Jackson Miller confided in me that he had never had much interest in reading because he didn't think there'd be anything to read that interested him. That conversation was a lightbulb moment for me. It was the first time I'd considered that kids who are not readers would not necessarily ever *think* to go find books about their interests! I would automatically think to go and get printed material about the things I love to do, places I want to go, and so on, but I'm a reader already. I'm wired that way. Jackson, and kids like him, aren't.

On the first day of eighth grade, I arrived at school before anyone else, or so I thought. I unlocked the main door and began mindlessly flipping on hallway lights as I headed to my room. I remember unlocking the door to my room and stepping into the darkness, my fingers searching for the light switch, when I heard a cough. A COUGH! *Someone was in my room.* I froze in place for a moment, then flipped on the lights and spun around sharply, preparing to defend myself with a Scholastic tote bag full of new hardcover books, a paperback copy of Avi's *The True Confessions of Charlotte Doyle* (which is *not* a book only for girls—it's murder and treachery on the high seas and so much more), and a stuffed Clifford the Big Red Dog that was within reach. Anyway, my heart nearly stopped beating when I saw Jackson Miller sitting at my desk with his feet propped up, looking like the cat who ate the canary! "Jackson! How in the world did you . . . Do you have *any idea* how early it . . . What are you thinking and why didn't you and how could you have managed . . . ?" I stuttered and stammered one unfinished thought or question after another, and he beamed. At last he got out of the chair and walked over to me and spoke through a sly grin. "Those Navy SEAL books you bought were pretty good, Dr. Layne!"

Mrs. Shapiro, my elementary school librarian, had the greatest impact on me as a reader when I was a kid. I was a squirrelly kid who could never keep still, constantly doodled on his paper, and would shout out answers instead of raising his hand. My third-grade teacher, who ran her class like an Orwellian dictatorship, had no use for me and no patience for my wily ways. She would lift me up by my ear, throw me out of the classroom, and send me to the library, effectively making me the librarian's problem.

And a problem I was. I hated reading in third grade, so the last place I wanted to be was at the library, but Mrs. Shapiro, who knew I'd eventually show up at her door, always had something for me to do. She would have me unpack the books, and let me pick which of the brand-new books I'd get to read before anyone else. She would handpick books for me from the collection, knowing which ones I would like. She made me feel special. At the beginning of third grade, I could barely read a picture book—but by the end of that year, I was reading Roald Dahl and Beverly Cleary.

Over the next few years, I became a fixture in the library. I was called down every time a new crate of paperback books arrived. I got to know the smells of the publishers. No kidding. My friends would blindfold me and then flip the pages of a new paperback in front of my nose, and I could tell them which publisher it was. To this day, I still remember the smell of *Journey to the Center of the Earth* and *Lord of the Flies*.

When I graduated from elementary school, I was surprised to receive the school's reading award and was told that I had gotten the highest score in the district on the standardized reading test. This from a kid whose third-grade teacher recommended him for special ed (which, back in those days, was called "the slow class").

On graduation day, Mrs. Shapiro came to me, tears welling in her eyes, and she said, "I've named each of my gray hairs Neal Shusterman."

I've tried to find Mrs. Shapiro, but no one seems to know what became of her. I hope she's still with us, and that I find her someday, so that I can give her a heartfelt "thank you." And maybe name one or two of my own gray hairs after her. My hair should only have such an honor!

—*Neal Shusterman*

CHAPTER 3

I Didn't Know They Still Wrote Books for Adults: Igniting a Passion Through Book Chats

There are only a few things that get me upset. One is driving behind a Pace community bus in our fair city. They stop every seven yards to pick somebody up or drop somebody off, and they are slow as molasses. I know people need bus service, and I'm all for mass transit, but let's spread those stops out a little! I will not drive behind a Pace bus; that's all there is to it. I simply refuse. I have nearly caused a fatal accident on countless occasions when I became trapped behind a Pace bus and had to initiate an escape plan. The number of people who refuse to ride with me is growing.

Another thing that really upsets me is when teachers are told by the school board that something new has been "added to the curriculum" but teachers are never asked to be involved in making the change (probably because they know we would ask what was going to be taken away from the curriculum to make room for the new addition). Take, for instance, the time a member of the school board entered my room (during instruction, no less) wheeling a cart full of bright, multicolored boxes. I halted my exhilarating discussion of conjunctive adverbs to inquire what all this was about.

"You teachers need to teach study skills!" a woman with far too much eyeliner and a fake mink stole trumpeted loudly as she forged her way to the back of my room. My head began to pound, and a vision appeared of me behind bars for making a bad choice while my class watched in horror and disbelief. "Where do you want it?" she blurted.

"Well, which box is mine?" I questioned with precision, a slight strain edging forward in my throat. I could feel trouble coming.

"What do you mean, 'which box'? They're *all* yours!" she exploded with enthusiasm. "The school board voted on it last month. We put it in your goals, you know. You teachers gotta teach more study skills. So . . . we bought you this great program."

I quickly thrust my pointer into the hands of a student intelligent enough to know why I was giving it away. "Well. What is it that *we teachers* will no longer be teaching while we teach what's in those boxes you have so generously purchased for us?" Of course, she did not have an answer to my question. They never do.

But what gets me worked up even more than Pace buses and crazy curriculum decisions is when I am with adults who start talking about the books that are "hot" right now. I never know any of the books they're talking about! Imagine being a professor of reading and literature and feeling left out of a book discussion group. It's humiliating! A book may be on the *New York Times* Best-Seller list, but if it doesn't start with the words "Harry Potter and the . . ." I surely will not know a thing about it.

You might say, "If this bothers you so much, read adult books. Then you won't be left out of all the conversations." And, yes, that would seem to be an easy fix. Except, I can't. I have become a reader hopelessly addicted to books written for children and young adults, and there's no going back. There's no self-help group, either. I'm not so sure it's the books that I'm addicted to, really (though they are tremendous and getting better all the time); I think it's actually what has happened again and again when I've put the right book in the hands of the right reader, or when I've known just the right book to recommend to a student who's convinced there's nothing she'd like to read. When I can do that, kids read; moreover, I feel like I *am* what I say I am—a teacher.

And so I read books for kids constantly, which makes it easy to forget that there are still people out there writing books for adults. This is my reality: I am on an airplane seated next to a man wearing an Armani suit, navy with thin pinstripes, and well-shined Florsheim shoes. I am wearing a sweatshirt that says "RECESS" in primary colors, and I have on my sensible air-travel tennis shoes. He is reading *The Da Vinci Code*; I am reading *Lily's Purple Plastic Purse*. I have learned that it is easier to say, "learning disabled." He looks at me, not unkindly, and that is the end of it. If I have in hand one of the many books I force myself to read because I know they will actively engage teenage girls—something like *The Sisterhood of the Traveling Pants*—the CEO sitting next to me looks at me repeatedly with contempt because he has decided that I am a perverted ex-con who will be back in the slammer within days. (I take comfort in reminding myself that he could well be married to the woman who wheeled that cart of multicolored study skills boxes into my classroom.)

Now don't misunderstand me—I'm not trying to rain on anyone's parade or criticize teachers' recreational reading choices. I'm not saying you have to be like me and give up Tom Clancy or John Grisham (or perhaps Patricia Cornwell or Danielle Steele). But in order to be true to the spirit of this book, I have to speak the truth of my experience. And the truth is that I can read a lot of books for kids in the amount of time it takes me to read one adult novel. Better yet, I have found I enjoy the kids' book much more than I ever did an adult novel. I know that each one I read could be the "just right book" for a boy or girl who could cross my path at any moment, and I want to be ready. A great goal to work toward, I think, is to be one of the people in the school building that kids come to for book recommendations—even when you aren't their teacher!

Sources Promoting Great Books for Kids

Once I gave myself over completely to reading children's and young adult literature, I needed help finding books. School and youth services librarians are great places to start, but there were times when I wanted to do the hunting on my own. I knew enough, as many of you do, to go to the American Library Association Web site and look up the Caldecott, Newbery, Printz, and Seibert medal winners, as well as the winners of several other awards, but I wanted to go beyond that. I wanted a day-to-day list to work from, something we had not focused on in my teacher training or advanced degree programs.

A whole lot of detective work led me to some powerful information that I have used to guide my career ever since, and I am excited to share with you a list I have compiled that has served me well over the years (see Appendix A). It is not my intention to provide an exhaustive list, but rather to share with you some of the resources I discovered that helped me find, read, and promote great books for kids. I'm hoping this list will take you beyond the top award winners that you already know about and generate excitement as you "freshen up" your reading lists.

Once I discovered all these resources, I read constantly. Then I found, quite by accident, the power I had to dramatically impact the lives of my students by putting them in touch with the right books—and I was hooked. It all began with Gary Paulsen's *The Transall Saga*. I had purchased the book after listening to Gary talk about how he didn't like science fiction novels, and, after writing one, he still didn't like them. That was enough to intrigue me. I started it on a Sunday evening, thinking I would preview, read a chapter or so, and head off to bed. I finished the book in one sitting—at 2:15 a.m. and showed up looking less than rested as the sixth graders pounded into my classroom on Monday morning.

I absentmindedly stood the book up on the far corner of my desk and busied myself with some paperwork. Suddenly, a voice inquired, "Hey, Dr. L—what's this?" I glanced up, noted Kyle pointing at the book, and made some comment about it being the source of my exhaustion. Long story short—one question after another followed until, by the time the bell rang for class to begin, every student was in a semicircle around my desk, listening intently as I answered their questions about the book. And I didn't get it. I didn't understand what was happening.

The same series of events occurred with the seventh graders. And *still* I didn't get it! When did I get it? (I do hope you are wondering that!) I got it when our librarian informed me that every copy of *The Transall Saga* was checked out of the library, that a waiting list had been established that might last into the next millennium, and that kids were still streaming into the library during every passing period. She encouraged me to warn her prior to telling kids about books in the future.

Some of you are not surprised by this at all, but I will tell you that I was speechless. At no point in my teacher training nor at multiple levels of higher education had a learned person ever said, "Read books written for the age group you teach and then tell the kids about the books." In other words, nobody ever told me to deliver short (five- to eight-minute) commercials for books to my students. No one told me (or taught me) to deliver book chats. And though it may sound ridiculous, I simply never thought to do it either. I read a lot of great books aloud to my classes for the first eight years of my career, but I never told my students about great books they might enjoy.

To further embarrass myself, I admit that during these early years of my career I was always in the front row at a conference or seminar where a speaker was talking about great new books for kids. I loved to listen to book chats, so I am dumbstruck looking back and wondering how it never crossed my mind that my students would love to hear someone talk about books, too.

Book Chats

Immediately following the events surrounding my impromptu book chat on *The Transall Saga*, I set off to test a theory. I arranged to deliver book chats in both elementary and high school classrooms (warning the librarians first, of course). Every book I highlighted in the chats was checked out, and a waiting list had to be created for each title. My head was spinning as I drove home from the high school. It couldn't be this simple, could it? How could something make such a dramatic difference in the motivation of readers and be such a big secret? It ought to be happening on a regular basis in every grade level at every school in the world, and yet no one I had ever taught with viewed it as a regular and necessary part of instruction. Most had never even tried it—of that I was certain.

My next step was to remove myself from the situation. I did not want it to be said that the book chats were effective because *I* was doing the talking. The case can easily be made that some people deliver a book chat more effectively than others just as some use more inflection when they read aloud or make eye contact more regularly when they teach; however, my goal wasn't to compare teachers. The goal was to determine whether the book chats were motivating to kids no matter who was delivering them. I asked some teaching colleagues if they would help test my theory by telling their classes about a favorite book written for kids, and they agreed. After alerting the library staff, my colleagues gave their book chats. As I suspected, the books they introduced were all soon checked out, and waiting lists were necessary.

I am so passionate about the need for teachers to give book chats on a regular basis in their classes that I look for every possible way to incorporate the issue into my speeches and consulting work. In the reading methods courses I have taught to undergraduates, book chat preparation and delivery is always a requirement, and those unfortunate enough to be assigned to me for student teaching supervision are required to give book chats during one of my announced observations. Despite having delivered them in the methods classroom, some student teachers were still very reluctant to provide book chats in the "real world." Sometimes they could not get past the idea that promoting a book in front of real kids might not work the magic I espoused, which is why I forced them to do it! The sense of empowerment that comes from watching kids scramble for books following a book chat is a tremendous confidence builder in new teachers, and its effect on veterans is rejuvenating to say the least. On my list of all-time best ways to stimulate a positive attitude, interest, motivation, and engagement in text with readers, providing book chats is at the top.

BOOK CHAT BINDER

One of the great benefits of discovering the power of the book chat is that teachers who think they have no time suddenly find they do have time—to read! What really happens, of course, is that we make the time to read because our students become so excited about reading that they are anxiously waiting for us to tell them about more books. Their motivation motivates us!

I have found that if I jot down a few notes in my own words when I add a new title to my book chat list, it helps me recall the characters and plotline more effectively than simply rereading the jacket flap. Also, a book may not be readily available in my room for a quick review prior to promoting it, so having something written that I can review before the book chat is very helpful. Figure 3.1 shows a filled-in example of a simple form I have used for several years to keep track of my reading and to help me prepare titles for book chats (a blank version is included in Appendix D). I always want to have some type of a hook that will capture everyone's attention and heighten interest in the plotline or characters, so I record that on the form first. I follow that up with some brief written notes on the plot, and then list additional titles the author has written that might be of interest to my students.

I keep these forms in a binder. My original binder grew to the point that I needed another one, which was very exciting, until one day I caught one of my students in the Bermuda Triangle and realized what a big mistake I was making with these binders. I had frequently told my classes that there were two Bermuda Triangles— the one on land (which is the lesser known) involves the triangular space behind my

FIGURE 3.1

BOOK CHAT PREPARATION SHEET

BOOK CHAT # _114_   **GRADE LEVELS** gifted late/ —(_2-3_)

TITLE: _Andy Shane and the Barn Sale Mystery_

AUTHOR: _Jennifer Jacobson_   **PUB. DATE:** _2009_

PUBLISHER: _Candlewick Press_   **ISBN:** _978-0-7636-3599-2_

HOOK: _Before students arrive, make large "price tags" on bright neon paper and place them on things around the classroom to give it a "sale" atmosphere. Ask what they think is going on. Discuss the 5 senses in terms of a sale._

NOTES: _twist on "gift of the magi" as Andy's idea to raise money (via Barn Sale) leads to trouble. Andy wants to buy a case for Granny Web's binoculars, but he has no $. During his barn sale, the binoculars accidentally sell. Andy sells his bike to get them back. Granny trades them for a new seat for Andy's bike!_

OTHER BOOKS BY AUTHOR: _Andy Shane and the very bossy Dolores Starbuckle, AS & the Queen of Egypt, AS & the Pumpkin trick, Winnie Dancing on her Own, Truly Winnie ..._

desk, an area where my private teaching materials are kept. I explain to students that stepping into that area often results in mysterious disappearances of students who are never heard from again. Most effective.

I kept the book chat binders in this area not so much because I considered them private but because there was shelf space, and I don't like clutter. I have recorded hundreds of titles in these binders—more book chats than could be given in a year, yet never once thought to make the binders available to the kids! Until one day, coming back from my lunch period, I caught a young man in the Bermuda Triangle with a binder in his hand. I had no idea what he had, at first; I jumped to the conclusion that it was test materials or some other type of contraband. When I called his name, I expected him to spin around and face me with the appropriate look of dread and fear. Instead, he looked up briefly, as though I was nothing more than an irritant, and resumed his hunt. I became unglued, things got loud between us, and he yelled, "Well, if you wouldn't keep these binders back here, maybe we could find out more about these books!"

I suddenly realized what was actually in his hand and simultaneously realized my mistake: I had been thinking they were *my* binders when all along they should have been *our* binders; they should have been out for my students to review. I made them available the next day, and students came running. Better yet, kids began asking me to give chats on specific books they found in the binders because my notes interested them, and they wanted to "really hear the whole thing." The work I was already doing—jotting notes to myself about books and throwing them into a binder—suddenly became yet another avenue to interest kids in books.

THE HOOK

The hook in a book chat is no different than having an anticipatory set for a lesson. Is it a necessity? No. Does it fuel enthusiasm, arouse curiosity, and add excitement? Yes. Hooks can be as simple as asking a question that you know ties to the plotline of a book you are about to introduce. When I introduce my young adult novel *This Side of Paradise* to teens, I often launch a discussion with them about cloning. "What if you lost your dog, Biscuit, when you were nine years old, and now someone could re-create Biscuit for you? Would you want him back?" This usually fuels a nice debate among teens. Then I ask them how they would like it if they discovered that their parents had "ordered them up" with a *preferable* color of skin, eyes, hair, musical talents, and athletic abilities. As the debate rages, I proceed to ask them what might happen if a father were to order up a perfect family before he figured out what he was going to do with the family he already had. That's a great question to launch a book chat on *This Side of Paradise*, a book I wrote to address the issue of just how close we might be, if the government allowed it, to having the ability to "craft" the perfect family for certain well-to-do citizens.

Effective hooks can simply be using an accent or adding a drawl to your speech, as I've been known to do when introducing Frances O'Roark Dowell's *Dovey Coe*, a terrific mystery set in the Appalachian Mountains. I am always careful to be sure my students understand that when my speech is altered it is not in an attempt to mock or poke fun at people of different backgrounds but rather to help the character(s) seem more authentic.

Costumes or simple props can make for great hooks, and they don't have to be elaborate. If I walk into an elementary school classroom wearing a plastic tiara and announce that my name is Nancy (to introduce Jane O'Connor's *Fancy Nancy*), believe me, I have everyone's attention. Likewise, if I turn out the classroom lights and turn *on* a flashlight—introducing myself as Joe Hardy and explaining that my brother Frank has gone missing while working on a case—everyone wants to hear more about it. We can even play twenty questions about the case Frank and I are working on, which actually puts the students in charge of the book chat!

TO EXCERPT OR NOT TO EXCERPT

There is no doubt that reading aloud an excerpt during a book chat generally adds great fuel to the fire. There are times, though, when sharing an excerpt is not the best choice. The decision about whether to read aloud an excerpt of text is one that should not be made in haste. I liken the choice to a craftsman selecting just the right tool for a very intricate job. If the wrong device is chosen, the entire project can be ruined.

Novelists will often talk about finding "the sweet spot" when it comes to reading aloud an excerpt, and when a new book is released we often agonize over finding that just-right place for weeks. The selection I want the audience to hear may be at a point in the story that would require too much explanation of back story before I begin the reading. Or my story might have several characters in the best scenes, but there simply would not be time to explain who all these characters were before I begin to read. Try reading an excerpt from fabulous whodunits like Ellen Raskin's *The Westing Game* or Agatha Christie's *And Then There Were None*, and you'll know what I mean. The beginning of a novel can be a great lead, at times, but in other situations the opening of a story may not supply enough information to truly engage the listening audience unless you read more pages than time would allow.

So what am I really saying about reading aloud excerpts during book chats? Use them as often as possible but utilize very strict criteria in selecting the passages. If you find a "sweet spot" that requires too much explanation prior to reading, don't use it. And don't expect that every excerpt you select will work the way you intended. You may need to try a few different places with kids before deciding on the one that really does the job. Of course, you don't ever want to read a passage without giving the needed information for your listeners to become interested. If you mention Fred in your excerpt and they don't know who Fred is, their minds will be on this unidentified character and not on the rest of the passage you are reading. There are no hard and fast rules on the overall length of a book chat, but I try to keep them six to eight minutes in length, which means that my excerpt is likely to be around four minutes long.

NARRATIVE VOICE IN BOOK CHATS

The most common and certainly the easiest type of book chat to give is one that is delivered in third voice or third person. Then it is simply me, the teacher, talking about the book. Certainly, there is nothing wrong with giving every single book chat from now until retirement in third voice; however, many of us have a creative streak that needs to be taken for a little walk now and then. I have found that altering the narrative voice I use for book chats spices things up a bit and makes them even more enjoyable for me to deliver.

For example, I might on any given day deliver a book chat promoting Margaret Peterson Haddix's *Among the Hidden* in any of the three possible narrative voices.

After using my hook to get everyone's attention, I might say,

"My name is Luke Garner. I've never been to a birthday party, I've never gone to school, and I've
never had a friend."

OR. . .

"Your name is Luke Garner. You've never been to a birthday party, you've never gone to school,
and you've never had a friend."

OR. . .

"His name is Luke Garner. He's never been to a birthday party, he's never gone to school, and
he's never had a friend."

As a matter of fact, delivering any of these three statements with a great deal of intensity in your voice could actually serve *as* your hook because the statements are so alarming. It is not at all difficult, I have found, to alter the narrative voice in which I deliver a book chat once I come to know the story well. This means that those of you who have regularly given book chats in third voice are closer to being ready to switch voices than you think. Try practicing a book chat that you typically deliver in third voice—one you know very well—but switch to second voice. Now the events will be happening to "you" and of course "you" is your listening audience of students. It is very gripping to be in an audience and have the teacher talk about the book as though you are the main character! I find it just as easy to move into first voice and tell about the story as though I am the main character. I do on occasion prepare a book chat in first or second voice right from the start, but there is no doubt that third voice is easiest. If you are an inexperienced "book chatter," keep in mind that switching narrative voice may be simpler for you once you have already had a lot of practice giving a specific book chat in third voice.

FROM THE TRENCHES

I remember well my great excitement as I drove out to a school one fall afternoon to observe Miss Callahan, one of my best student teachers ever. Today, she would be giving book chats to her students (I had, of course, insisted), and I would be videotaping her as part of our university's requirements. She would then have the opportunity to watch herself at work on tape and reflect, in writing, on her delivery and impact.

Last spring, Miss Callahan had given two phenomenal book chats in my methods classroom. She brought the house down and left no doubt in any of our minds that children would be wild for books once she was done talking about them. To see her today in action with real students, I reminded myself, was one of the reasons I so loved the supervisory part of my job. I bustled through the school hallway with such anticipation as I have rarely known. As I entered the room, I greeted the students who knew me well, and then gave Miss Callahan a thumbs-up sign. She had the video camera ready and waiting and so, at her nod, I began filming. She then stepped to the front of the classroom and began delivering a book chat by reading aloud from an index card! I felt chest pains immediately and hoped an oxygen mask would fall from the ceiling—as should happen in certain emergency situations despite the absence of any aircraft. Miss Callahan looked and sounded like a robot! There was no trace of the bright and charismatic girl who had delivered book chats in my methods classroom the spring before.

My choices were clear: the children and I could all die from boredom before the first book chat ended, or I could take some kind of action to stop this insanity. I could think of no way to signal her, and so I was forced to do the unthinkable. I had never, ever, interrupted a student teacher during instruction, but desperate times call for desperate measures.

She stopped her reading when I approached her and demanded she hand over the note cards while the students looked on in utter silence. She was dumbstruck. "What?" she squeaked in a voice that might belong to the world's tiniest church mouse.

"Miss Callahan, give me those note cards—every last one of them." Though my tone was no-nonsense, I hoped that my eyes spoke quiet comfort, and I mouthed, "You can do this." She passed over the cards with trembling hands, and I proceeded back to my seat.

"Dr. Layne," her voice quivered, "what should I do now?"

"Tell your students why you like the book, Miss Callahan," I said with confidence. "I believe it *is* one of your favorite books, is it not?"

She began to speak about the book and after two anxiety-filled sentences she forgot herself and became lost in talking about a story she dearly loved. She read aloud a great excerpt that led some children to cry out from their desks with excitement. All the books she talked about disappeared from both the school and classroom libraries that day. A couple of days later, Miss Callahan stopped by my office at the university. She wanted me to know that her students were already asking when she would be giving her next round of book chats. I'm proud to say she already had a date picked out.

The morning period in third grade when our teacher, Miss Gerow, read aloud was a magical time for me and for everyone in the class. I remember vividly how the atmosphere in the room tingled with anticipation and excitement as she displayed the cover of the book she had selected. Then, she effusively introduced the author and the illustrator, promising us that they would be our guides throughout the story and our friends forever afterward.

The light in the room seemed to glow more brightly, and Miss Gerow (who was in actuality rather diminutive) took on heightened stature as she grandly ushered us into the opening of the story. Reading as dramatically as if she were auditioning for the leading role in a major theatrical production, she proceeded to enchant us with the sounds, the sights, and the wonders of the unfolding narrative.

My love of stories, pictures, and books soared throughout that third-grade year in 1949, and I am deeply grateful to Miss Gerow for her determination to send us off with that gift, and for the fact that it has continued to enrich my life during all the decades that have followed.

—Steven Kellogg

Don't Bother Me, I'm Busy Changing Lives: Igniting a Passion Through Effectively Reading Aloud

I tell them on the first day of class, which is a lot like boot camp, by the way, "*I'm a new teacher to most of you. I remember what that was like when I was in school, and the question always hanging in the back of my mind was this one: What will get me in trouble with the teacher? Well, none of my teachers ever answered that question for us. Finding out was trial and error. You, ladies and gentlemen, are fortunate because I'm going to answer that question for you. Right from the start. Day one, here we are, and you're going to hear it straight from the horse's mouth. There are only four ways to get into trouble with this teacher. Number one: cheating. This category encompasses copying, plagiarizing, doing someone's homework, providing a look at your homework to someone else—you get the picture. It's a broad category. My advice—when in doubt, don't. Number two: lying. This category includes white lies; whoppers; omissions of the full, complete, and unadulterated truth; general falsehoods; and so forth—another rather broad category to avoid at all costs. Number three: bullying. Strong persuasion supported by the use of fists, mean-spirited talk, or any type of handwritten note and/or electronic form of communication can easily be mistaken for bullying by me. When in doubt—don't. Number four: interrupting me when I'm reading aloud to the class. This category, dear students, is deceptive. It sounds less dangerous than the others and yet, those who have had the great misfortune to interrupt my read-aloud time (and lived to tell about it) would utter a single word of warning: BEWARE! You may interrupt me, and thus incur my wrath, by poking the person next to you, pulling the person next to you, whispering to the person next to you, and fidgeting. Also to be avoided as much as possible*

*during read-aloud are leaving the room, entering the room, crumpling paper, blowing your
nose, coughing, and breathing loudly."*

Of course, the vocabulary and intensity of this speech is scaled back if I'm working with little ones, but even they don't miss the message: read-aloud is serious business. And why shouldn't it be? It's one of the few literacy practices endorsed univer-
sally by researchers as well as those practitioners who regularly employ it. In fact, I'd
wager there's more agreement that reading aloud to kids is a solid literacy practice
than almost any other we could name.

Importance of Read-Aloud

Many who had already discovered the power and magic of this practice were over-
joyed when, in 1985, *Becoming a Nation of Readers: The Report of the Commission on
Reading* identified reading aloud as "the single most important activity for building
the knowledge required for eventual success in reading" (Anderson et al. 1985, 23).
This same commission identified reading aloud as "a practice that should continue
throughout the grades" (51). And yet, it does not. Encouragement to continue reading to children throughout their school career comes from respected researchers
and writers such as Stephen Krashen and Charlotte Huck, passionate authors and
speakers like Mem Fox and Ralph Fletcher, and, of course, America's foremost authority on reading aloud, Jim Trelease. Still, according to a study of read-aloud practices across the United States by Hoffman, Roser, and Battle (1993), the number of
practitioners reading aloud to students in our schools drops off markedly after grade
four. As I've talked with teachers across the country about why they aren't reading to
their students, their responses generally fall into one of three categories: (1) reading
aloud beyond grade three is not supported by the administration as a valuable use
of instructional time; (2) there's too much curriculum to cover already, so they cannot make time for reading aloud; and (3) they are unaware of the benefits of reading
aloud and the power the practice holds for promoting a lifetime love of reading.

The most efficient way to address such responses is to educate everyone—
administrators, teachers, even parents—about the benefits of reading aloud. I'm
convinced that when people understand the power of the practice, they will remove
barriers, make time, and commit themselves to reading aloud forevermore.

Benefits of Read-Aloud

The benefits of reading aloud, such as increased reading comprehension, improved listening skills, and a broadening of vocabulary, are commonly cited by read-aloud advocates, and there is no doubt that they make for very compelling and persuasive reasons. But I'd like to consider what reading aloud has to offer in terms of its contribution to building lifetime readers. In terms of our disengaged readers, those who can read but don't, being read to is one of the most seductive (yes, that *is* the word I intended to use) methods of bringing them to books. To reach these kids, we're going to have to impact the way they *think* about books and the way they *feel* about books. Right now, they're saying, "Books—not for me." We need to put them in a situation where being with books is pleasurable. What could be more pleasurable than a great book read aloud by a passionate reader? Add to that a terrific environment (see Chapter 7) and the lack of an assignment connected to the read-aloud experience (such as building the setting of the story out of Q-tips in a shoe box or writing an essay exploring the main character's motivation), and you have fired up a plan for engaging your once-disinterested readers.

Here's a reason for reading aloud to kids: it's fun! I know it's not very academic-sounding, but that doesn't keep it from being the truth. A good book read well will do more for the woes of our disenfranchised readers than all the leveled books the publishers can crank out. I know it because I have lived it. This does *not*, by the way, mean that I am against leveled books. I am in support of most ventures in reading education to some extent or in some form, with moderation (the exceptions being celebrity-authored children's books and school boards, both of which have nearly led me to impale myself on a sword repeatedly and with great force).

Think, for a moment, about the kids who don't "do" reading. For such children and young adults, very little about school actually *is* fun—because how much of school is *not* about text? The last time I checked, math was reading. So were social studies, science, Spanish . . . need I go on? This is why kids who don't "do" reading love recess and P.E.! Any place they are less likely to run into text is a *safe place*.

But when my teacher or the librarian picks up a great novel, a picture book, a poem, or a short story, and I know that when he or she puts that text down again I will not be asked to darken the oval that best describes a minor character, make a color-coded story map based on six literary devices, or find a song from a CD by a band the teacher's actually heard of that supports an underlying theme—then I can actually *enjoy* being with text. Please read the preceding sentence over several times to be sure you get the point. If I'm a disengaged reader, the knowledge that I will have an experience with text in school that will not be assessed allows me a unique opportunity that school rarely provides for kids like me: the chance to experience a good book read well. If we can't make kids read (and we can't), then shouldn't we be concerned about monitoring how often we're providing experiences with text that are enjoyable so that they might consider reading on their own? Reading aloud—a good book read well—is the number-one way to positively impact the disengaged reader.

Another great reason for reading aloud to kids is to broaden their interests and tastes. It's time to fess up. Let's start with me. I am not intrinsically motivated to read nonfiction books. Okay? There. I said it, and it may start a scandal and reduce my credibility nationwide in the field, but I don't think I'm too terribly different from most of the people reading this book. You might fill in the blank with a different genre, but most of you have one you could have contributed—a genre that you don't necessarily reach for right away. Maybe for you it's fantasy or historical fiction.

Now don't go running down the hall to your librarian saying, "Did you hear the news? Steven Layne hates nonfiction books!" That's not at all what I said. I have read many terrific nonfiction books in the past several years, but I did so because I made the conscious effort to seek them out and read them, not because I was drawn to them. In grade school, I was the kid who entered the library and heard the fiction section calling aloud to me, "come running and let your imagination soar." It's still that way today for me. I like to *imagine* a possible truth.

My lovely wife, Debbie, is the exact opposite. Don't bother her with a bunch of made-up drivel; she can't be troubled too often with an imagined truth—she wants the *real* truth, the facts, in a well-written and concise version without a lot of frou-frou. Can she read fiction? Yes. Does she, on occasion, read fiction? Yes. Does she *reach for fiction* first? No. And that's okay. Within our overarching genre of choice, there are plenty of categories to keep us busy reading. Debbie can read biographies, autobiographies, and informational or inspirational text. I can read historical fiction, fantasy, science fiction, and contemporary realistic fiction. We've both also learned, through deliberate choice, that there are great reads outside of our preferred genre, and so we go there on occasion—purposefully. We want to remain broad and deep readers—and that's what we want for our children and for our students.

The conscious choice of reading aloud from a wide range of genres is certain to broaden the interests and tastes of our students because many of them have failed to explore multiple genres. There's nothing wrong with having read all sixty-two books in a series; however, the literary world can be a bit skewed if that's the extent of a child's genre explorations. I'm ever convinced that some fourth grader is destined to discover that he loves fantasy books or a sixth grader that she loves historical fiction *this year*! Could it be that this is the year that the fire is intended to be lit in some reader's life? Will second-grader Bobby find out he loves sports fiction books, will he discover that such books even exist, all because a brilliant teacher who couldn't care less about baseball herself reads her class one of Matt Christopher's books? And will Chelsea, who's in eighth grade and has never been much of a reader, buy her own copy of Neal Shusterman's *Unwind* and stay up half the night to complete it because she can't wait for her teacher to finish reading it aloud in class? I'll just bet Chelsea's teacher is smart enough to tell her, when the girl confesses what she's done, that there are other books by Shusterman in the library; I'd lay odds Chelsea will be in the library before she catches the bus home. But did this young lady *know* she liked science fiction before her teacher began reading that book aloud?

For many years, I have used the same textbook—*Children's Literature, Briefly* by Michael O. Tunnell and James S. Jacobs (2008)—for teaching my undergraduate children's literature course. It is a favorite of mine for reasons that, were I to begin listing them, could take up the rest of this chapter. Quite some time ago, I asked for permission to alter a flowchart they produced in that book to better meet my needs, and the authors graciously agreed. I am eternally grateful that they have allowed me to provide my altered versions for you in this book, but I will have you know that the foundation came from them and from their great book.

I advocate providing these charts on cardstock to every student in the class as well as hanging a giant-sized version in your classroom for all to see. What I like about the charts shown in Figures 4.1 and 4.2 is that they allow us to kinesthetically interact and think about what we are reading. I teach my students to place their index fingers at the far left side of each chart and ask themselves if the piece I have read aloud is poetry, prose, or drama. We discuss the meaning of those terms. From there, index fingers move along the chart to the next question—is this piece fiction or non-fiction?—and so on. We continue to question and discuss together. We use these charts for any text I read to them, and, eventually, they can begin to use them for their independent reading (which will be recorded in their reading logs; see Chapter 5). On the back side of these genre charts, I provide definitions of every genre (Figure 4.3), which is a tremendous help to the students—especially at first. Obviously, teachers who work in the primary grades will want to stick to using the simpler chart (Figure 4.1), and they will need to adjust the genre definitions to match.

FIGURE 4.1

GENRES OF LITERATURE CHART

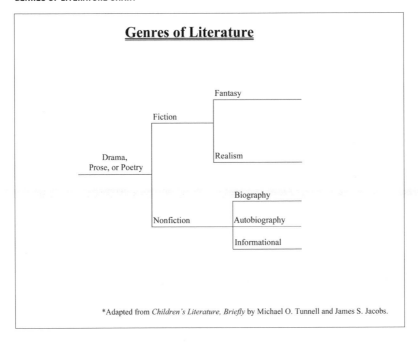

Genres of Literature

*Adapted from *Children's Literature, Briefly* by Michael O. Tunnell and James S. Jacobs.

FIGURE 4.2

GENRES OF LITERATURE CHART

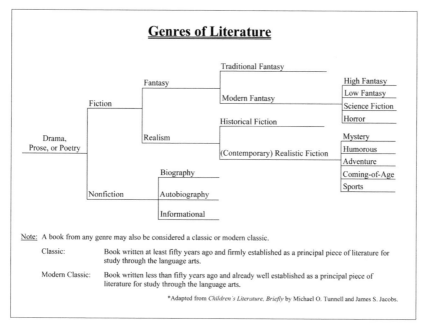

Another genre chart that I have fallen in love with was developed by Dr. Constance L. Marks. Or, at least that's what it said on the faded purple ditto sheet I discovered behind an old bookcase in a school library in Michigan about ten years ago. All of my attempts to track down Ms. Marks have failed over the years. If you know her, tell her she's brilliant, that I gave her credit for her work, and that I tried to find her. Have her give me a call. Her circular genre chart, shown in Figure 4.4, provides another way to view the genres that I find highly engaging. Again, this chart could be made tactile by allowing kids to highlight or color different genres as they are read aloud by the teacher or independently read for class. Titles and numbers of pages could be creatively woven into this chart as well. One teacher took my advice and made a large version of this chart—all white with black letters—and hung it on the wall outside her classroom. As the year progressed and she read aloud from different genres, she added colored pieces, cut from construction paper, over the white spaces. She reported back that the kids found this very exciting.

FIGURE 4.3

READING GENRES

POETRY   Written verse that does not appear in paragraph form. Poetry may be written in stanzas; however, it may also appear in columns, in shapes, or as a single line.

NONFICTION—BIOGRAPHY   Factual information is presented about the life of an individual; however, the information is prepared by someone other than that individual.

NONFICTION—AUTOBIOGRAPHY   An individual writes factually about his or her own life experiences.

MODERN FANTASY (LOW)   Story that deviates from the natural physical laws of the earth. Something happens that is not truly possible; however, the setting of the tale remains on earth the entire time.

MODERN FANTASY (HIGH)   Story that deviates from the natural physical laws of earth. Something happens that is not truly possible. The high fantasy tale is set in, or on, another world; otherwise, the story begins on earth and the principal characters are transported to another world in some manner.

TRADITIONAL FANTASY   Stories and tales handed down from long ago that have no known author. When they were finally written down, it was by "collectors" rather than authors.

SCIENCE FICTION   A specialized branch of modern fantasy which deals with scientific possibilities. Sci-fi often takes known scientific facts and promotes new and unproven possibilities with them. These stories can sometimes have a futuristic depiction of life on earth as part of the story line.

HORROR   A branch of modern fantasy in which the plot revolves primarily around monstrous creatures and/or gruesome events meant to arouse fear in the reader.

CLASSIC   Written at least fifty years ago and firmly established as a principal piece of literature for study through the language arts.

MODERN CLASSIC   Written less than fifty years ago and already well established as a principal piece of literature for study through the language arts.

HISTORICAL FICTION   Tells the story of people from a time period that is not considered today's world. Generally has a strong historical backdrop against which the lives of the principal characters and the plot are played out.

CONTEMPORARY REALISTIC FICTION   Tells the story of people during a time period that can be considered contemporary—happening in today's world.

FIGURE 4.4

CIRCULAR GENRE CHART

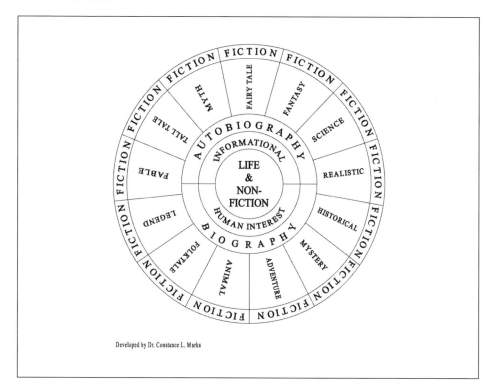

Developed by Dr. Constance L. Marks

We teachers must not underestimate our role in the great reading puzzle. The conscious choice not only to read a good book well but also to choose our read-alouds with intention so that we are covering a wide range of genres may make all the difference for some of our students. We must realize that the decision to expose our students to books from many different genres can be a significant factor in helping them discover that there may, in fact, be a kind of book that really lights their fire. Reading aloud is our best vehicle not only for exposing kids to the various genres but also for delivering those genres in a powerful and exciting way that will, hopefully, nurture a desire in our students to ask where they can find "another book like the one you just finished reading to us."

When I was a brand-new teacher, just out of school, I taught fifth grade in a terrific school in Carpentersville, Illinois. I was charged with teaching a unit on the Holocaust and encouraged to use Lois Lowry's book *Number the Stars*. In this particular school district, at that time, students were ability grouped for reading. Guess who was given the lowest-ability reading group? It's a miracle novice teachers stay in the field. Their classrooms are robbed of every decent piece of furniture before they arrive. The overhead projectors in their rooms are taken and replaced with the old dinosaurs that always show the image crooked on the screen, and then we give them the lowest-functioning group of children. But, hey, it was a long time ago. Water under the bridge. I've forgotten all about it. Almost. Okay, back to Lowry's Newbery Medal–winning historical fiction novel.

For those of you who have not read this brilliant masterpiece, *Number the Stars* is set during W.W. II in Nazi-occupied Denmark. It follows the story of Annemarie Johannsen and her family as they strive to save their neighbor's daughter, Ellen Rosen, from the Nazis who are hunting for her. By story's end, Ellen is safely across the sea to Sweden. I was not sure exactly how best to go about teaching this novel to my low-achieving fifth graders but decided we should begin by having a brainstorming session on World War II. Some of you are already laughing out loud. STOP IT! I was young and new. I thought I had it right. I had a giant piece of butcher block paper hung on the wall and those flavorfully scented markers were at the ready. What more could one need? Well, I won the Guinness Book of records prize for the world's shortest brainstorming session. There were absolutely zero contributions. Nary a marker was uncapped! I realized then that kids can't brainstorm prior knowledge when they don't possess any. Did I mention that the principal was in the room for the first formal evaluation of my teaching career? Ahhhh, memories! Another time.

The important discovery I made throughout the next two months as I read aloud from this story was that reading aloud, and the discussion that surrounds the story, builds background knowledge. My students learned a lot, not only about the Nazis, but about Germany and Denmark: geography, customs, history, language, religion. For example, when they asked if Denmark was the only country the Nazis invaded, I obviously told them that it was not. This led a team to research—self-initiated research! That group reported back on all the other Nazi-occupied countries, which led to a discussion of how Germany could manage it all, which led to my telling them that Germany had help—the Axis Powers. Well, another group was off like a rocket to research the Axis Powers, and once they reported on that, we had to have a group report on the Allied Powers. And so it went. I smile to myself even as I write these words, remembering such classroom moments. This is why I became a teacher!

I'm not sure that everyone realizes the tremendous amount of background knowledge that can be built through the read-aloud process, regardless of the genre. True, on the surface it might appear that historical fiction would build *more* background knowledge than certain other genres—fantasy, for example. One could argue that *The Lion, the Witch, and the Wardrobe*, *The Book of Three*, and the Harry Potter books do not build useful background knowledge because they are set, in large part, in worlds that do not exist. I would argue that a very significant kind of background knowledge is built when such stories are read aloud. As students learn, via their teachers, how to navigate a fantastic world and the accompanying text successfully, aren't we contributing to a knowledge base that may, in fact, help them to navigate or appreciate other literary works certain to come their way in later years, such as *The Iliad* or *1984*? My answer would be a loud and resounding YES!

Every story read to students from any genre contributes to building their background knowledge in some way. I say this because if there's one thing I have confidence in, it's teachers. No teacher I have ever known reads aloud a book to kids and fails to stop and discuss something now and then. We don't do this because some manual tells us to; we do it because we have good brains and a teacher instinct that tingles and tells us it's time to stop and talk. It's our own special superpower, and nobody else understands it. Because reading aloud is such an intimate act, the conversations that take place surrounding the book being read matter; they matter a lot, and the kids remember. If it wasn't true, I wouldn't have had fifth graders trying to read their siblings' high school history book chapters on World War II.

Living with four children of my own, I have learned the value of improving a child's listening skills. Though their ability to listen can, on occasion, be impacted by rewards and/or threats, my favorite way to improve their listening skills is by reading to them. Students in my classes, even at the university, are no different; everyone wants to listen to a good book read well.

In the elementary and middle grades, it is important for us to capitalize on the difference between a child's listening level and the silent reading level of the same child because, in most cases, there is about a two-year difference in these levels. In other words, the fifth grader can listen to text at about a seventh-grade level and comprehend it, even though silently reading the same text might prove troublesome. Until the latter part of eighth grade, most students working at grade level or below have listening levels that are significantly higher than their silent reading levels. It is obvious that we must always make responsible decisions regarding content when we are selecting text to be read aloud; however, when we are reading aloud from text beyond a student's listening level, we are actually bringing him more mature vocabulary, more sophisticated literacy devices, and more complex text structures than he would meet in text he could navigate on his own. The last time I checked, this was called good teaching.

Reading aloud not only provides an opportunity to improve students' listening skills, it also affords teachers an opportunity to reinforce targeted reading skills. Let's say I am reading aloud to a group of second graders. I may stop and ask how a specific character is feeling at a given point in the story. If the character is angry, but the textual clues are all evidenced in the character's behavior as opposed to specific statements made in the text, I have a great opportunity to reinforce the skill of inference. Calling on my students to identify the character's emotional state and asking them to support their position will undoubtedly lead to a discussion of story clues plus real-life knowledge, which opens the door for me to shout "inference!" The story will be under way again in no time, and students won't even realize we had a skill lesson—but we did. To underestimate the value of the teachable moment I just described could be a serious mistake; through the read-aloud, I may be reaching kids who most need skill reinforcement. I'm convinced that some of their brains turn to mush the moment we power up a projector, take out a worksheet, or ask them to open up their workbooks. Some of them can smell a skill lesson coming a mile away, but the scenario I just described is teacher stealth at its best. Most of them will attend to the entire conversation—eager for us to return to the story—and remain blissfully oblivious to the fact that learning was taking place.

Now don't go running down the hall to the principal saying, "Steven Layne says workbooks are bad!" If that's what you got out of this, you've missed the whole point.

I'm not down on projectors, workbooks, or any other tools of the trade. I just want us to be aware that in some cases, such aids can be a warning signal to kids of what we have planned. I prefer subtlety as my first line of attack. The more direct forms of instruction are also fine, and I will use them—just not always as an opener.

We've all heard the saying "attitude is everything" and though it's cliché, it's also true. A good book read aloud well tends to foster positive attitudes toward books in general. I don't know about you, but I've lived through enough quick-fix sermons to last me a lifetime. Why anyone who has ever worked with kids would suggest that if we just buy this one product, enact this one initiative, or listen to this one speaker, every child will become a reader is beyond me. I'm all about incremental movement along the reading attitude continuum because I believe it more accurately reflects something that we need to be more focused on in schools: real life.

The continuum in Figure 4.5 shows polar opposite attitudes and behaviors with regard to books and reading. I can't understand why anyone would believe that if we purchase Accelerated Reader, everyone is going to move all the way from the far left to the far right. STOP! Don't go running down the hall screaming, "Steven Layne hates Accelerated Reader! It says so right here in his book!" It's easy to read what we *want* the author to be saying. Some will be disappointed to hear that I believe Accelerated Reader has value . . . for some kids. How can I not believe it?

Imagine that we have a colleague standing before us earnestly saying that she or he has students who are excited about reading because they *love* the AR program. Can we say, "No! You are wrong about these students you work with every day. Though we do not know them or work with them, you have to be wrong because what you are saying does not fit with our position on AR!" It would be insane and professional

FIGURE 4.5

READER CONTINUUM

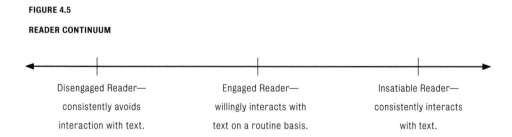

Disengaged Reader—	Engaged Reader—	Insatiable Reader—
consistently avoids	willingly interacts with	consistently interacts
interaction with text.	text on a routine basis.	with text.

suicide to say such a thing. Plus, how could a person like me say such a thing when in first grade I was motivated beyond words to get to "aqua"—the final color in our classroom SRA kit. Some kids in my first-grade class still couldn't get the box open by the end of the year, and others didn't even know we *had* an SRA kit! (I *was* the *first one* to make it all the way to aqua by the way. Not that it really matters. But I was first.)

Mrs. Porter, my first-grade teacher, wisely told me long ago that something works for every child. "I just made it my business to have a lot of 'somethings' in first grade," she said. Her wisdom flies in the face of all who embrace the idea that if we just do, buy, or promote this "one thing," it will all be made right. In order to take a student from the far left position of "I hate books, I don't read, and you can't make me," we are going to have to put him in a position where being with text becomes enjoyable; we are going to have to impact his attitude. A good book read well does that brilliantly! Those who know me well know that I can get a bit feisty at times (blame my mother). Those who know me *really* well know that the issue of reading aloud to kids is one that I am quite passionate about, so the feistiness tends to show itself when anyone states, implies, or delicately hints at the idea that there might not be time to read aloud to kids in school.

I would just *love* to know (see, here I go), how these individuals think we are going to get kids who won't read to want to read if they are never around texts that are enjoyable. Kids who don't do "the reading thing" need to be exposed to great stories being read aloud well. When they walk into the classroom saying, "You're going to read some more of that today, right?" we are starting to see a bit of movement on the continuum. The goal isn't to fly them from one end to the other. The goal is movement in the right direction.

One of the most frustrating things to me about our educational system is how little attention is given to helping kids make the connection between what is being learned in school and how life works in the real world. Take, for example, coding books with colored dots in school, which is, in some cases, entirely out of control. I understand and applaud the philosophy of trying to help kids get "right fit" books; however, some people who take a plan to the extreme—like color-coding books and assigning kids to a color—may be doing more harm than good.

I was doing some consulting work recently in a certain U.S. state. I was told by a school librarian that she had been explicitly instructed by the superintendent to close the library for one month (keep in mind this is *during* the school year) so that every book could receive a color-coded sticker. She was then told that, when the library reopened, she was to be sure she was checking each child's reading classification (available on the school Intranet) prior to allowing any books to be checked out. She said to me, "He then told me that if I checked a blue-dot book out to a red-dot child, my job would be in jeopardy." This librarian had several colleagues standing with her, verifying the facts of her story. I smiled and responded, "Ladies, think what great training this is for the students. Now they'll be able to walk into Barnes and Noble out in the real world and simply identify themselves by saying, 'I am a yellow-dot person. Please take me to the yellow-dot books.'"

Reading independence is not promoted by scenarios like the one just described. When I read John Grisham's first book years ago (back in the day when I actually read adult books), I immediately got another John Grisham book. Why? Because my parents had modeled for me; they had certain authors whose work they read. I learned from them that most authors write more than one book, and, while there are no guarantees, the odds are good that if you liked one book by an author you'll probably like more.

Though I had many wonderful teachers, I don't recall any of them ever promoting the concept of *author* to the students. Actually, the verb *promote* does not rush to mind either when I think of my school experiences with books. We read what was assigned. We went to the library once each week. If we checked out a book, fine; if we didn't, fine. I can't shake this dream I have of kids going to the bookstore or library and having some idea of what they are looking for prior to arriving there. How does that begin to happen?

Let's say I am reading aloud *Tough Boris* by Mem Fox to the second grade, *The Kidnappers* by Willo Davis Roberts to the fifth grade, *The Rules of Survival* by Nancy Werlin to the eighth grade, or *Counterfeit Son* by Elaine Marie Alphin to the tenth grade. When I am done, I'm heading straight to the library—or I'll use my classroom library if necessary—and I will be sure the kids all see and hear about any other books we have available by these authors. We must teach our students this simple concept: If you liked one book by Chris Crutcher or Barbara Park, you might like more. Too few kids know who is writing the books they enjoy, and it may be that the reason they don't know is either because we aren't telling them or because they aren't expected to know.

I read aloud a wide range of books to my kids at bedtime, and believe me, they know who the authors and illustrators of those books are. When I read aloud in a classroom, the same is true. I make a big deal of reading the author's name and, if applicable, the illustrator's name—every time. If I am reading aloud from a chapter book, students are going to hear "And now, *The Giver*, by Lois Lowry," every single day. My seventh graders used to moan, "Okay, Dr. Layne! We know it's by Lois Lowry! You don't have to say it every day!" And I would respond, "YES, I DO! Because when I'm done with this sweet piece of literature, you're all going to remember who wrote it. Got it?"

When we, as educators, make it our business to teach not only books but also authors, we can move forward with regard to creating a more educated society. I don't know about you, but that's why I enlisted.

The final, and perhaps most important, benefit that comes from reading aloud to kids is that lifelong readers can be developed. One of my favorite questions for preservice teachers has always been, Which do you want: students who can read or students who want to? Of course, I am hoping they will come up with "both" as an answer. When we finally get there (sometimes it takes longer than other times), I remind these educators, "if you want both, then teach like it."

In other words, don't just assume that because kids can read, they will read. The skill and the will are two very different things; we need to acknowledge that fact, and then we need to teach as if we understand that fact to be true. The problem, in my mind, is that will is the oft-neglected piece of the puzzle. Too many times, reading instruction is exclusively centered on imparting the skill of reading. Will is an afterthought for many teachers who aren't trained in this area and, consequently, are unsure how to address the more intangible attributes of attitude, interest, motivation, and engagement.

The intention of this book is to put a tool in the hands of teachers who aren't sure exactly what a classroom looks like where teaching the love of reading is considered part of reading instruction. Of all the strategies discussed in this book, a good book read well is the number-one method. Don't let anyone tell you differently; it will just make me mad.

FROM THE TRENCHES

The practice of reading aloud is a regular component in many of my speeches across the country, and I hear from new converts frequently. In fact, I recently received an e-mail from a middle grades teacher who had heard me speak on the topic and decided she should try it. Her e-mail to me at the end of her school year began, "You have made me a hero in my school and with my students . . ." I did not make her a hero. I simply educated her, convincing her that she had the ability to make a significant contribution to the reading lives of her students. And it worked. She was surprised, but I wasn't. I've seen and heard the stories as teachers make what I call "the great discovery" time and time again. And each time I hear one of these stories, it takes me back to when it first happened to me.

I was a brand-new teacher with my first class of fifth graders in Carpentersville, Illinois. I was terrified to begin working in a school that did not have the best reputation. Two stories I had heard from friends who had substituted in the building had to do with fifth graders throwing desks across the room and second graders stealing from the teachers. I opened class on that first day with a story, and those kids were mine for the rest of the year.

Near the end of our time together, I decided that we would make a quilt of their greatest memories of fifth grade. We'd had some excitement that year, including a trip to an amusement park and a big pizza party. As they brainstormed the greatest moments of fifth grade and I recorded them all on the chalkboard, I noted that book titles were popping up frequently. Over the next few days, we whittled our list down to the top twenty-four moments so that each child could depict one on a quilt square. I noted right away that every book I had read to them that year made the cut. Interesting, I thought. Then, one student asked if we could rank order the list from the best moment of fifth grade on down. I saw no purpose, since each of our top twenty-four would be on the quilt, but the class was so enthusiastic to rank them that I finally agreed.

My students taught me a lesson that day, and I promised them not only that I would never forget it but also that I would share it whenever I could. With no guidance from me, the class unanimously voted my reading of Madeleine L'Engle's Newbery Award–winning *A Wrinkle in Time* as the finest moment of their fifth-grade year. It wasn't the trip to the amusement park. It wasn't the pizza party. It was a story. Because many of my students did not have a lot of material possessions, I had assumed that something more tangible would take the top honor. What I learned that day was just how tangible the intangible can feel. I love the way Mary Lee Hahn puts it in *Reconsidering Read Aloud*, "Read-aloud may look like an ordinary event in a typical classroom, but it feels extraordinary when the teacher who is reading is aware of the power of the book and the importance of (his)/her role . . ." (2002, 1). On that day in early June 1990, a group of fifth-grade students taught me the greatest lesson of my teaching career: never underestimate the power of a great book in the hands of a teacher who knows how to use it.

Most teachers can probably remember the one teacher who had the power to inspire and empower, the teacher who most greatly influenced him or her to become a teacher. For me, it was my fifth-grade teacher, Mrs. Kathadaza Mann, a strong black woman who taught us to be proud of our heritage as well as our capabilities. She was the first to deeply influence my love of learning and teaching. Mrs. Mann was truly powerful—boldly speaking for us who did not yet know how to speak for ourselves. From her, we learned so much more than math and spelling. She taught Black History long before it was politically correct or socially acceptable and loved all her students, both black and white. And she read literature to us—Shakespeare, Thoreau, Hughes, and Dunbar—and we loved it and learned it because no one ever told us we couldn't. She challenged the accepted

standards to prove to us we were wonderful, and we believed her. She gave us the power to dream, and the inspiration to believe we could accomplish anything.

Several years ago, I actually got the opportunity to thank her at a teacher breakfast sponsored by Scholastic at a National Council of Teachers of English conference in Orlando. Scholastic provided a limo for Mrs. Mann and her husband, both in their eighties. We brought her on stage, and in front of several hundred teachers, I gave her roses and hugs, this poem, and my deepest gratitude. She said she remembered me! But even if she didn't, I will never forget her. She is the reason I became a teacher.

—*Sharon M. Draper*

TEACHER

I was ten and full of wonder
Anxious then for school to start
With red plaid dress and brand new crayons
Fifth grade dawned to grab my heart.

Our teacher met us at the door
How low and silky hummed her voice
A mystery of books and chalk dust
She offered challenge, change and choice.

She wore pearls and silky dresses
Laughed and cheered each sweet success
Marched with us to higher visions
Never stooped or stopped for less.

Cloakroom hooks and home for lunch time
Days of hot and cold extremes
Games for math and bees for spelling
Fifth grade memories, magic, dreams.

With a smile she taught us patience
Whispered secrets breathed us strong
Words and rhymes and tales of beauty
Filled our minds with joy and song.

Through her wisdom we dreamed visions
Of fruits of pride and hope's moist vine
Because of her life, I am a teacher
Touching lives as she touched mine.

From *Teaching from the Heart* by Sharon M. Draper ©1999.

CHAPTER 5

My Modeling Career: Igniting a Passion by Reading with Students

I could never make it as a model. First of all, I don't do a pouty look well. Second, I always blink at the wrong time. Finally, and most important, I could not tolerate the minute-to-minute concern over food choices. When I am hungry, I prefer to eat—often ordering something that tastes good and that I would enjoy eating. Such is not the career of a model, I feel quite certain.

Fortunately, in the kind of modeling that I have been successfully involved with for several years, none of the aforementioned conditions are a concern. The gifted reader has already predicted that I am speaking about modeling reading for my students. A question I try to ask myself on a regular basis is this one: Do my students know I love reading? They may know that I *teach* reading, but that's a very different issue. How would you, as a reader, answer these questions: Do your students see you as a reader? If someone came to interview them concerning characteristics about you that rush to their minds when they describe you, would "reader" and/or "books" come quickly from their mouths?

As with many of the strategies and suggestions in this book, modeling yourself as a reader is neither time-consuming nor difficult. The hardest part, I think, is making the conscious effort to write it into your lesson plans. For readers who are thinking, "Sounds great, Steve. What exactly does this look like in the classroom?" let me be more concrete. I know when I first came up with the idea that I needed my students to see me as a reader, it took some time for me to figure out just exactly what that *would* look like in the classroom.

Book Stories

I began by making a list of stories about books and me. I don't mean I wrote short stories, I just jotted down some phrases that would immediately bring a specific story about books and me to my head. Here's an example. When I was a kid, I loved reading mystery stories: Hardy Boys adventures, Agatha Christie novels, even Nancy Drew (yes, I was a closet Nancy Drew reader, buying them from the local bookseller for "my sister." I am an only child). When I shared with my students that most of the world believed there were only two Hardy Brothers, Joe and Frank, but in actuality there were three—Joe, Frank, and *Steve*—they were amazed. I told them how we three brothers solved every mystery together and how I could hardly wait to read the next adventure when I was a kid. Later on I fessed up about Nancy and took the obligatory ribbing—but suddenly we couldn't keep Hardy Boys and Nancy Drew books on the shelves in our school!

Not all the stories I shared were from my childhood. I told book stories from early in my teaching career, too. And each time I finished a story, there was a new run of "hot" books that kids were after in the school. When I told the story of how L'Engle's *A Wrinkle in Time* had so powerfully connected with the first class I ever taught, all our copies were gone from the library. My new students were not about to be outdone by my old students!

The Teacher's Hot Read

Another type of effective modeling comes into play when I make it clear *that* I am reading by promoting *what* I am reading. Let's say you are teaching second-grade students. If you want to spark reading in those kids—try this suggestion for one year and just see if it doesn't make the difference for many of them.

Get a book stand (see your librarian for help if needed) and place it in a prominent location on your desk. Next, create some kind of attention-getting small sign (hang it from the ceiling, maybe? Display it on your desk?) that says, "Mrs. Hager's HOT Read!" (See Figure 5.1.) (If your name is not Mrs. Hager, please feel free to alter the sign accordingly.)

On that book stand, you will place a book that you are currently reading—one appropriate for second-grade students. This should not be a book you are reading aloud to the kids. That is a totally different book being read to them for a totally different purpose. This book is *your* book, one you are reading for yourself but written at *their* level. You are reading it during SSR, you are reading it for a few minutes when there is in-class work time (so that they visibly see you reading), you are taking it home at least two nights a week and reading some from it (and your students will check to see what page you are on so if it goes home, you better be reading). Within days of this book's appearing in its prominent location on your desk, you will begin to hear "chatter" from kids who may have already read it—telling other kids and/or you about it. You are also bound to have kids coming to you asking what chapter you are on, how you like it so far, do you have another copy, does the library have any copies, and can this copy be checked out when you are done? Obviously, if you are teaching in the primary grades and reading picture books, you will move through them far more quickly, but this simply generates that much more excitement in your young readers.

FIGURE 5.1

My Dream School

In my dream school (where I am principal, everyone has to do it my way, and I can never be fired), every adult working in the building must be reading a book written for one of the grade levels of students our school services. All these adults—the nurse, the secretaries, the custodians, every teacher and teacher assistant—have signs that say "Mr. Tanner's HOT Read." (The art teacher made them for the whole school—willingly—bless her soul!) Everyone's book is on a stand. (The librarian ordered stands for the entire school with money supplied from one of my you-never-knew-it-existed principal budget accounts—bless her soul and mine!) You see, in my dream school it is not possible for a student to encounter an adult who cannot tell them about a great book. We are, so to speak, "in their faces" with books at every turn of the corner.

   I truly subscribe to the belief that everyone working in a school is someone's hero; everyone is the right person and, in some cases, the only person to reach some kid with a book. Thus, we need every adult reading books for kids. If you want to work in my school, you either get on board with this plan, or you simply can't stay. I know it's a dream, but what if it came true? What would happen to reading scores over a three-year period? What would happen to library book checkouts? What would the impact on kids' attitudes be like? I keep espousing my plan to crowds, hoping that one day my phone will ring and some incredible leader will say to me, "Come on over, Dr. Layne! The whole building is on board for a three-year commitment to become your dream school!" You see, this is the perfect plan because I would be helping to institute the framework and to keep the momentum up in my dream school—but I couldn't be fired because I wouldn't actually be the principal!

Reading Logs

I wrestled with calling this section "Reading Logs" for fear that some of you would skip over it thinking you already knew what I was going to say. After all, the term *reading log* is not some newly coined moniker, and I'm not about to say that my version of it is significantly better or more effective than one that many of you already have in use. What may be different and what is most important to me is the *way* the reading log is actually used.

Figure 5.2 (also in Appendix D) is a sample of a reading log I designed and have found to work effectively with kids. It is not time-consuming to complete or cumbersome to carry, nor does it require too-busy parents to lie by signing their names each week to guarantee that their children have read *x* number of pages. We usually update these logs each Friday at the first opportunity. I update mine as well—in front of my students. When or where time and space permit, I advocate a giant-sized replica of the log that fills an entire bulletin board so that kids and any visitor to the classroom can't miss seeing what the teacher has to say about what he or she has been reading (kids' books only, here—don't be writing up your adult novels).

FIGURE 5.2

Reading Log Selections

Name _____   Grade _____

Qtr	Title	Author	Genre	Rating

I record the title and author as well as the genre, and then I give the book a one-to-five-star rating. That rating is key because it will influence some kids to go after a certain title. The genre category is also extremely important because, since I force myself to vary the genres constantly, I model what I preach to my students. If I say that I want them to become broad and deep readers, I must do the same.

I believe most everyone has genres they are drawn to and those they avoid. There's no shame in it; it is often simply a fact. My students have always known that non-fiction has never been where my heart lies. You can bet that once I reveal that, my students are all over me if they don't see a nonfiction title on my reading log about every five or six books! The other strength in teachers' purposefully reading from multiple genres and rating them on this public reading log is that students can look at titles from *their* favorite genres on the teacher's reading log, consider the rating the teacher gave it, and head down to the library to make a more informed decision. For example, if I give a nonfiction title a five-star rating, you can bet it's going to get a lot of attention in the library because the kids already know nonfiction is not my genre of choice. If I'm giving that title five stars, my students who love nonfiction are going to trample one another to get their hands on that book! And you know I have read so many wonderful nonfiction titles simply because I exposed the truth about me as a reader—and my reading selections—for all to see.

While it might seem that recording the title and author are more mundane, perhaps less useful, but altogether necessary components of the log, this information is beneficial in more ways than you might initially consider. When it comes to students' wanting to recommend titles to friends, the ability to flip through to this log and name the book and author becomes a real time saver.

Listing the titles also interrupts the tape some kids play in their heads that says, "I'm not a reader. I don't read." Each Friday, when we are updating our logs, I encourage everyone to record everything they have read in the past week: in-class short stories, poems, a column in the newspaper, an article in *TV Guide*, a comic book, directions for using a new iPod—*everything and anything counts!* In fact, a Tootsie Roll may come flying across the room to the student who identifies the most unique "out of the box" text read in the past week. That type of promotion keeps everyone thinking harder about the reading they have done. It also honors the many types of text students read. Some of you have already realized that the more types of text we acknowledge and record, the more quickly the log gets filled up! I am all about saving trees, but this is one time I don't photocopy back-to-back. I want the kid who plays the tape in his head "I don't read" to have to come up to me and ask for another log because his is full. The more often he has to do that, the more frequently that pesky tape is being interrupted, which is one of my key objectives as a teacher.

Just as listing titles is important, so, too, is the identification of the author and/or illustrator. Though I mentioned it just a few pages back, it bears repeating. I want you to actually do something about this problem! I go crazy over the number of people who want to recommend books to me but have no idea who wrote and/or illustrated them. How can we grow educated citizens in our schools when they don't have answers to the question, Who are the people who write and illustrate the kind of books you enjoy reading? This is where a skills-only approach to reading disappoints us. When our exclusive focus in schools is on teaching students how to read, our success may breed young people who can read but who don't necessarily have a desire to read. And if they do want to read, has their school experience taught them anything valuable in the way of helping them know how to find something they would enjoy? If we've taught a group of students to read, but none of them can readily identify favorite authors or genres, I'm not sure how much we've accomplished.

I'll never forget a sixth-grade girl who couldn't remember the author of a book she was recording in the log, saying, "Does it really matter who wrote it?" I may have scared a few years of her life away between my verbal hysterics and my physically climbing the walls of the classroom in response to what she considered an innocent remark. May I just say this to every teacher and student in the world: YES, IT MATTERS WHO WROTE IT AND WHO ILLUSTRATED IT! Kids don't seem to have any trouble knowing they want a shirt produced by Abercrombie & Fitch. They don't forget that they want a Facebook account or an iPod, so I'm betting if we raise the bar a bit in our schools, they'll be able to remember the names of the people producing books they enjoy.

Previews

I have recently begun telling audiences that I wish there were a hidden camera monitoring me whenever I begin to read some new text. Every time I start to read a new book, I find myself modeling exactly what I have taught kids to do—and exactly what I have encouraged other teachers to do: effectively preview the text prior to officially beginning to read it.

I love to tell students that previewing a book (or any text) is a bit like becoming involved with a mysterious puzzle. Nearly every kid likes to solve a mystery, so this is an effective hook. When I preview, I tell them, I make it my business to find every scrap of information possible about the text before I begin any "official" reading. I ask myself, How much can I figure out about the text in advance? It's not just teacher jargon when I discuss effective previews with kids, it is a process I believe in and follow religiously in both my personal and professional reading. The following areas of focus allow me to model and discuss with students the previewing process I go through prior to reading. I will describe it in terms of a book, but any type of text could apply with slight adjustments as needed.

Title: How hard would you think about the title of your first book if you were an author? Have you looked at the title of this book and truly realized how long and hard someone probably thought about the title? Do you think the author intended this title to be silly? Scary? Mysterious? Can you rate this title on a scale of 1 to 5 with 5 being really great?

Author/Illustrator: Look at the name(s) of the creator(s) of this book. Do you recognize the name(s)? If this is an illustrated book, have you ever seen or read other stories that have the same look as this one? What does the information on the back jacket flap have to say about the author and illustrator? Is there a Web site listed? If not, you might Google the author's or illustrator's name and see whether he or she has a Web site you could visit to learn more about this book.

Dedication: Do you know how to find the dedication in a book? On what page is it usually located? What is the purpose of the dedication? Some dedications don't tell us much as readers. For example, if the dedication says, "To Bonnie," we don't get much insight. But if the dedication says, "To Anthony for making us giggle on the bus," we can wonder about what that means and make some predictions—especially if this story has to do with a bus or with laughter!

Front Jacket Flap: The front jacket flap is where the plot summary is located for a book. Do you know that most people say to read the back of a book to find out what it is about—and they are wrong! The one consistent place to find out what a book is about is the front jacket flap. All books have a plot summary there that usually will not give away too much of the story—just enough to get the reader interested.

Cover: We all have heard the saying "Don't judge a book by its cover," but we still often are guilty of doing it. Is your book a picture book? If so, the cover is likely to be the same picture as one on the inside of the book. If that is true in this case, why do you think the publisher and author selected that particular picture from inside the book to reproduce on the cover? Was there a better choice in your opinion? If the cover is *not* a reproduction of one of the inside pages, why not? Should they, in your opinion, have reprinted an inside page instead of going with a whole new picture for the cover? If your book is a chapter book, someone was usually paid well over $1,000 dollars to design the cover. How hard would you work for that kind of pay? Would you design your cover to give the readers some hints about the story? Do you think this cover designer tried to give you any hints about the story in the design of the cover?

CIP Page: Many times on the copyright page of a book, you can find what is called the CIP or Cataloging-in-Publication Data from the Library of Congress. This information provides a one-sentence description of the entire story. While it can be a great help during a preview, it can also give away the end of the story and ruin the surprise for you. It's important to know that this information is available because there are times when a one-sentence summary can really help you decide whether a book is the right choice for you; however, I usually choose to skip this information when I preview a book. I don't want to know too many secrets in advance.

Back Jacket: Just what exactly does go on the back of a book? This is the most exciting part of the mystery of previewing because the answer to this question is: you never know! There are so many different ways the back jacket of a book is used. Sometimes it contains remarks from readers or critics about the story; there could also be an excerpt from the story or a listing of awards the author has won for his or her writing. Other times, the back jacket might contain information on a totally different book written by the author or other books in a series to which this book is related. There might be graphics on the back cover that suggest something about the book or graphics that are just completing the artwork from the front jacket. It is exciting to see what the back jacket of a new book will offer us as we try to figure this book out before we read it!

Chapter Titles: If this book is a chapter book, review all the chapter titles. Which is the most interesting? Once you've decided, discuss with a partner or small group to see whether any of you picked the same chapter! Argue your point to see whether you can convince anyone to give up their chapter title and agree that yours is more interesting. Try this for the funniest chapter title, the scariest, the most mysterious, and so on. You can also make your own categories for reviewing chapter titles.

Interior Graphics: Are there any type of drawings, charts, or graphs in this book? If this is a picture book, go on a quick "picture walk" by flipping through the pages and seeing what you can gather about the story line prior to reading. If this is a chapter book with interior graphics available, select two or three to look at carefully and consider what they seem to indicate about the text.

Shopping

The ability to conduct an efficient preview of text will be a tremendous help to students in all content areas, especially if we make them aware of the benefits inherent in the activity. A strategy I simply call "shopping" makes excellent use of my students' abilities to preview text and leads many students who are normally uninterested in text to interact with books willingly. By modeling and discussing with students how books are marketed by publishers and how I shop for books, I am actually teaching them a life skill that can serve them well as consumers in both libraries and bookstores.

I love bookstores and libraries (big surprise, I know). But I am a realist, too. I know that many students avoid these locations whenever possible. The main reason, as discussed earlier in this book, is that they have no idea what they are looking for if and when they do enter. Again, teaching kids how to find a book is not really part of the curriculum. The furthest I've seen a school district go is to train kids to enter and say, "I am a yellow-dot person, please point me in the direction of the yellow-dot books." Such children and young adults are sure to grow up and be a lot of fun at parties. If you need me to further explain my feelings about the color-coded "dotting" of both books and human beings, please reread this entire book while completing all the pages labeled *inference* in the deluxe worksheet accessory kit. Please note: the blue kit is for those of you who are really smart. The green kit is for those of you who are smart enough to sit really close to people using the blue kit. The gray kit is for those of you who make really super paper airplanes.

Figure 5.3 (also in Appendix D) shows a form I have used for many years in the primary-grade levels. We call it our "Someday Book List," and place the cover of my good friend Denise Brennan-Nelson's book *Someday Is Not a Day of the Week* at the top to remind us to make these books a priority. In the intermediate grades on up, I simply call it "Books to Consider" (Figure 5.4; also in Appendix D), and I have students use it for a variety of purposes. The point is not so much how it looks but how it is used. I've already made clear in Chapter 3 the importance of book chats, and you can see a section on Figure 5.4 designated for that activity. When my students are listening to book chats presented by anyone, they are required to have this form on their desks. They don't have to write on it, but it has to be there. I plant the suggestion that if they hear about a book they might want to read someday, they should record it now in the book chat column.

FIGURE 5.3

FIGURE 5.4

Books to Consider
From Shopping: _____
_____
_____
_____
_____
_____
_____
From Book Chats: _____
_____
_____
_____
_____
From Recommendations: _____
_____
_____
_____
_____
From Read Arounds: _____
_____
_____
_____
_____

The top section of this form is provided for shopping. Now, anyone who has ever heard me speak knows that the level of admiration and respect I have for librarians is immense. My Canadian friends often use the term *teacher-librarians*. I am in love with the sound of that because it emphasizes that they are, in fact, teachers. While it is certainly possible to host a shopping trip in your classroom, a well-stocked, regularly weeded school library is the ultimate place for a shopping trip—and this means working collaboratively with the librarian. You can double what can be done for kids if you work with your librarian to ignite a passion for reading. The finest librarian I ever had the privilege of working with is Kathy Dickson, and the smartest thing I ever did was to enlist her support as I sought to reach kids who, in some cases, seemed unreachable.

STEVE WITH HIS FAVORITE LIBRARIAN, KATHY DICKSON

Let me set the stage of what a shopping trip might look like for one of my sixth-grade classes. First, Kathy and I have worked out that she will take a large number of great books (multiple genres and reading levels) from the shelves and set them up on tables all around the room. These will be only hardcover books because paperbacks have no book jackets, which means some of the information I have taught my students to use in a preview is not available.

Back in the classroom I am readying the troops. They have their Books to Consider sheets (grades three and up) in hand or the more generic Someday Book Lists (grades K through two), and I have them lead me in a quick verbal review of what we have learned about how to find a book. They will, of course, brilliantly list all the possibilities for previewing text that were discussed earlier in this chapter as would be appropriate for their grade level. At the conclusion of this quick review, I will tell them that we are heading to the library where they will use their previewing skills to shop for books they might want to read someday. There are sure to be kids who are already reading a book. I want to plant the idea that we are building a list of books for the future. I describe what the library will look like before we enter and ask them to remain totally silent for the first ten minutes we are in the room. At the conclusion of ten minutes, they can talk, recommend books to friends, check out books, and so on. The next fifteen minutes or so is a very social time focused on books and sharing, and Mrs. Dickson and I are always heavily involved in discussion during this time.

The first time I took a group of students shopping at the library, they were asking when we were going to do it again before I even got them back to the classroom! Over the years, I have had the opportunity to work in a variety of schools and take kids of all ages on shopping trips. The enthusiasm is always high. For the primary students, I like to have some volunteers in the library (parents, other staff members) so that we can record titles for the little ones if it is too difficult for them. I love to see book titles being recorded on those shopping lists, and I relish the thought that, in the future, we could be sending kids to the library who actually have a book in mind they would like to read. This beats the typical scenario many librarians face as a student wanders into a room with 9,000 books and says, "Hey! You gotta book that's sorta like that one book I read one time?"

Researchers have reported it for years—kids need to see adults reading. Big shock? Probably not. Do these adults who keep preaching to kids how important reading is ever model reading for the kids? It's great when kids can see their parents reading; however, we can't control that. I have tried always to remind myself what I can control, and one thing I have ultimate control over is whether my students actually see me reading. I know the guilt some of you feel when you read in school. I won't for a minute deny that I have felt it, done battle with it, and even lost that battle once or twice—shortening the reading period I had planned to get back to work. It's scary to read and maybe even (gasp!) enjoy it for fifteen or twenty minutes when you are "supposed to be teaching." Right? And yet, folks, the research has told us that kids need to see reading modeled. I want to challenge you to make an instructional decision for the coming quarter, semester, or year: decide on an amount of time your students are going to witness you reading and stick to it. I don't care if it's two fifteen-minute periods a week, or daily for ten minutes, or only on Friday for twenty minutes, but take charge and make a commitment. Then, I want you to ask the kids a few months later, How do you guys feel when you see me reading while you're reading? What do you think of that? Should I be grading papers instead? Do you think I'm not doing my job? If your experiences are anything like mine have been, you will receive a lot of reinforcement for reading from the kids.

I was visiting with a former student recently, and she made this comment. "You know, Dr. Layne, what I remember the most about school was your reading." I smiled, thinking that she was referring to books I had read to the class, and I asked her which had been her favorites. "Oh, no," she said, "I didn't mean the books you read to us. I loved them all. I could name them, but I was thinking about just watching you read books at your desk or on the floor while we were reading ours. Lots of teachers had told me to read before, but I'd never had a teacher who actually read when we read." She grinned and confessed, "I used to look up from my book sometimes and just watch you reading yours. You were so into it. You were captivated by books. I didn't know that word back then, but now I know that was what was happening to you. I remember that I wanted to be just like you, and now, thanks to you being my reading role model, I am."

I am going to have to cheat a bit on this assignment. First, I have to write about two teachers. Second, neither of these remarkable educators ever worked with me in a classroom or assigned me a book to read. However, each of them absolutely electrified me with the power of story.

The first was my grandmother, Lillian Feldman, who taught elementary school in Brooklyn. She must have been amazing at it: according to family legend, when the district attempted to assign her to a different building, the parents at her school staged a massive walkout. Grandma stayed put. Anyway, I have two favorite memories about my grandmother. She made delicious homemade kreplach soup when I was sick or sad, and she read me Roman and Greek myths when I was bored. Unfortunately, the kreplach recipe died with her, but I internalized the recipe for the myths: *try to explain the world in story, and you end up explaining humanity instead*. I also learned that if you can get a kid to associate reading with love, that kid will never, ever stop reading.

The second was Denis Kiely, the owner of the sleepaway camp I attended in the Pocono Mountains of Pennsylvania. He taught high school history in Valley Stream, New York, and was also a practicing lawyer. And a former head lifeguard. A former city councilman of Long Beach, New York. A champion wrestling coach. The most masterful person I've ever met. At camp, we had Quaker meeting every Sunday morning, at which campers and staff could stand up and

 speak as the spirit moved them. Mr. Kiely told life-changing stories there; my favorite was a traditional yarn he told once a year about the difference between Heaven and Hell. One Sunday when I was fifteen, I was walking next to Mr. Kiely on the way to the service and asked him whether he was going to tell the Heaven and Hell story that day. He stopped walking, looked me in the eye, and said, "No—*you* are!" The lesson: *kids can tell amazing stories if you give them a real forum and a real audience*.

I've been a very lucky student; the New York City public schools taught me well. My high school creative writing teacher was Frank McCourt. Yes, *the* Frank McCourt, who taught me how to turn my stories into novels and, thus, gave me a career. But I wouldn't have had the stories in the first place if not for the lessons I'd already learned on my grandmother's floral couch and in the woods of Pennsylvania.

— *Jordan Sonnenblick*

CHAPTER 6

Can We Talk? Igniting a Passion Through Book Discussions

Can we talk? Comedienne Joan Rivers made this question famous, and I have had a lot of teachers pose the same question to me. They're not asking if they can talk *to* me (though at times people do want to talk to me); rather, they're asking for my professional opinion about whether they can talk *with* their students. In essence, their question is, "Do you think it's a good use of instructional time for us to allow time for and take part in discussions about books?" Given the current emphasis on accountability in schools, it's a legitimate question. Conscientious teachers are asking whether just about everything their gut tells them to do is actually a good use of instructional time. Certainly, allowing students to sit around and talk about books could be suspect by the instructional-time police. How will we *know* they're talking about books? How will we *assess* the quality of their discussion about books? What will the consequences be for not talking about books when we say they're supposed to be talking about books? Opportunities for infractions abound.

For those who love a sense of order, and I readily include myself in this group, the whole notion of let's sit around and talk about books smells of a lack of structure, a sense of looseness, if you will, that can threaten the sense of order and decorum we stay awake at night trying to convince the world is needed in most every situation. I'll admit it was a long time coming for me—the idea of allowing such discussions without creating a structure that, in the end, we all hated and that stifled the very kind of discussion I thought should be promoted. The good news is that eventually, through much trial and error, I found a way to let it happen vibrantly and successfully for most every student.

Buzz About Books!

The best decision I ever made was to stop trying to grade or assess these types of discussions with my students. As you have read in the earlier chapters, I advocate putting a lot of things in place to help match "the right reader with the right book" (Lesesne 2003). One way to all but guarantee stronger discussions about independent reading choices is by doing everything we can to get kids the right books in the first place.

I realize there can be some confusion when I begin talking about book discussions because some readers will wonder if I am talking about books used for literature circle discussions, novels selected for whole-class book study and discussion, and so on. Let me be clear. In this particular chapter, I am focusing on students' independent reading selections; in other words, everyone in the class is quite possibly reading something different—something that has been self-selected. I might have any number of things happening in my classroom, but there has always been an expectation that, in addition to our major unit of study, kids are doing some independent reading at home (not every night necessarily) and in school (with time I provide). It's important to me to honor the text they are reading independently, and some time scheduled for book discussions without the trappings of assessment has worked brilliantly. I decided long ago to call these book-discussion sessions "Buzz About Books."

As with most everything discussed in this book, readers can alter my suggestions to suit a particular building, grade level, time frame, and so forth. I tend to *assign* students to discussion groups at the very beginning of the year, so there is some degree of incentive for kids to keep moving forward in their books. If students are in groups with their best friends, they can cover for one another more easily than will happen otherwise. Failure to be engaged in independent reading is not typical when kids are being matched with the right books; however, the reality of discussing what's happening in your story with peers who aren't necessarily your best friends can keep some kids motivated to move forward in their books simply because having nothing to say in their discussion group makes them uncomfortable. As the year progresses and kids get hooked by the reading bug, I often begin letting them create their own discussion groups.

When kids gather together in their groups, the meeting time is generally about fifteen minutes. Groups are sized at four, ideally; I go to five rather than three so that when there are absences the group can still have enough members to feel functional. My objective as the teacher is to join a group and remain with them for the entire discussion session—moving to a new group next time. At the beginning of the year, I often will circulate in an effort to be sure groups are getting off to a great start. Within a couple of weeks, though, I am certain to be a full-fledged participant in the process, which means I don't simply sit in with groups and observe or listen; I participate.

The most miraculous thing I have done to make these groups functional is to supply a focus item for them to discuss when they meet. They know that they can spiral their discussion off in any direction—ask one another questions or whatever—but having a focused topic with which to open the discussion helps everyone become more active participants. Figures 6.1 and 6.2 provide a complete list of the topics I have developed for these book discussions. For younger readers, topics can be adapted as necessary from my "Buzz About Books!" discussion starters (Figure 6.1). Teachers working with older readers can select from the large number of samples I have provided (Figure 6.2) without much need for alteration and reuse many of these throughout the course of the year. Each focus topic is broad enough that it can be easily discussed, despite the fact that every student is likely reading a totally different book. When a group meets, they can move in any order. I leave all of that up to them. Each student in turn will show the group the book he or she is reading so group members can begin to become familiar with the cover. The student will then identify the title, the author, and the page number he or she is currently on and rate the book from one to five stars thus far. Once this brief information has been provided, the student will address the focus topic with regard to the book he or she is reading.

Occasionally, I will have students freewrite about a focus topic for a few minutes. I may then have them share their writing in groups orally or turn it into a carousel, with everyone's piece moving around the groups for silent reading. At other times, I ask for volunteers to read orally for the class. I have been known to collect the writing at times and just read through everyone's piece to see how things are coming.

FIGURE 6.1

BUZZ ABOUT BOOKS—YOUNGER READERS

1. Where and when does the story take place?
2. Who are the main characters?
3. What is one of the main characters like?
4. Who is your favorite character and why?
5. Which picture in the book do you like best?
6. Which part of the story do you like best?
7. How do you feel about the end of the story?
8. What do you remember most about the story?
9. Do you think other kids would like to read this book? Why or why not?
10. Would you read another book by this author? Why or why not?

FIGURE 6.2

BUZZ ABOUT BOOKS—OLDER READERS

1. Identify something about the main character that's bothering you or something that you really like. Why do you feel the way you do?
2. What is the major problem in this book so far, or what do you think it is going to be? How will it likely be solved?
3. Select a minor character in this book and explain why you feel the character was created by the author. How would the story change if this character were removed?
4. Explain the setting of your book. Is it really important to the story line? What would change if you moved the story to another planet, a different country, or a fantasy land? Would the story still work well?
5. People are motivated by many different things. For example, some people will do anything for friendship, others for chocolate, others for revenge, others for money. What is it that you believe motivates the main character of your book? Explain why.
6. Identify the climax of your story. How did you know when you had reached this point?
7. Does your book seem to have a theme? In other words, do you think the author is trying to

---

communicate with you, the reader, through this story? If so, what is the author saying to his or her readers?

8. Describe a character from your book using three descriptive adjectives. Then, compare the character to yourself or someone in your family. What are the similarities and/or differences?

9. If your book has chapter titles, identify the most interesting title and explain what makes it so fascinating. If your book does not have chapter titles, describe some recent events that you've read about in the book and ask the group to help you develop a chapter title for that part of the book.

10. Read aloud for your group the inside jacket flap and/or back cover (if it has information about the book you're reading—sometimes the back cover contains information on another book!). Discuss whether you feel the publisher has done an effective job of convincing people to read the book based on this information. What do your group members think?

11. Which of the five key levels of conflict (man versus man, himself, society, nature, supernatural) are present in your book so far? Which conflict seems to be the main one at this point in the story?

12. If your book were going to be made into a movie, which part would you want to play? Why? Which would be the most enjoyable scene in the movie?

13. Discuss the book jacket (front and back) of the book you're reading with your group. What are people's opinions about how well the jacket "sells" the book? Having read some of the book already, can you suggest a better jacket idea?

14. Discuss an example from your book of a specific literary device that the author used well, such as foreshadowing, comic relief, or flashback.

15. If you've read any other books by this author, talk about how this one rates in comparison with the others. Can you tell it's the same person writing? What are similarities and differences between this book and others the author has written?

16. Compare one of the main characters in your book to a main character from one of your favorite books. Which one would make a better friend in real life?

17. Select any character in your book and rate him or her on a scale of 1 to 5 (5 is high) based on each of these qualities: dependability, intelligence, and appearance.

18. Talk about the resolution of your book. Did the author tie up all of the loose ends? Would you predict or even enjoy a sequel?

You can see that with these groups meeting two or three times a week for a few minutes, with my joining groups, and with the opportunity to write and share free-writing, there is a kind of built-in incentive for kids to give books a chance. Students can easily become convinced that we—their teachers— have read every book in the school just because they see us reading, promoting, and enjoying books. And when we randomly join the discussion groups, students are not very likely to make up the plot for fear we may pop into their group on that day and expose them. Also, because they talk about the same book for a few weeks with the same group of students, it is hard to fake progress. Other kids will catch on if a student says he is on page 46 and three days later says he is on page 33! I do want to stress that for these reasons—the looming possibility of my randomly joining groups, the students' desire to look good in front of their peers, and the considerable energy I expend matching kids with those "just-right" books in the first place—attempts at deception during book discussions have rarely occurred in my classes.

Status of the Class

Using the "Buzz About Books!" activity in oral or written form generally takes up fifteen minutes of class time three days a week. On the other two days, I usually employ an activity that is a bit less time-consuming and faster paced. I call it Status of the Class, and it is designed to do just what it says—give me a quick status check on where everyone is with their independent reading as well as allow every student in the room the chance to hear and see what their peers are reading. I train the kids to move through this like lightning. After a couple of weeks' practice, a group of twenty-five sixth graders should be able to complete this activity in less than ten minutes.

As always, I am a participant in the process, which means that I have my independent reading book (appropriate to the grade level) ready to show everyone. I keep a class roster sheet handy so I can make quick notes if necessary. The Status of the Class activity often begins with me because I want to continually model for them how quick the pace needs to be. I will stand where everyone can see me, hold the book out to allow everyone a good look at the cover, and simply identify the title, author, and page number I am on, then give it a one- to five-star rating thus far.

Sound familiar? It should. This is the preliminary information kids are sharing in their discussion groups each day before getting to the focus question.

While this might strike you as redundant, let me explain the rationale because the benefits are substantial in my opinion. First, identifying the title and author of a book they are reading each day is not terribly taxing, but it does increase their own familiarity with the work. It's tough to be able to discuss or recommend books in the future when you can't even remember the title and author of something you've read. I'd take the bet that many times our students don't notice the name of the author of their books, short stories, poems, and so on even once—let alone speak it aloud daily. The same can be true of book titles.

Another benefit of providing this information during "Status" is that this time the entire class is hearing it; in other words, it has a new audience. I have seen it happen so many times: when the girls all see and hear that Kendra is reading *I'd Tell You I Love You but Then I'd Have to Kill You*, by Ally Carter, suddenly that book is hot. Why? Kendra is popular with a lot of the kids, so now that they clearly see and hear what she is reading, that text becomes as popular as she is. I don't mind capitalizing on Kendra's popularity to advance the cause of literacy and neither should you. And don't think it works any differently if the title is Sara Pennypacker's *Clementine* in third grade. As with nearly every other strategy discussed in this book, grade level doesn't much matter. It's a few "tweaks" in the hands of a good teacher, and we're off and running. I've frequently watched some of my more gifted readers paying close attention to what other kids who are "like them" are reading. They listen attentively to the ratings their fellow geniuses are giving certain books and use those ratings to guide their own future selections.

Some of you may be saying, "Okay. I see benefits of title, author, and rating, but what is with the page number? Who cares what page they are currently on in the book?" If you think the page number is of little to no concern in the eyes of their peers, you would be absolutely correct. I'm the one who wants to know what page number they are currently on! I generally record that along with a quickly abbreviated title next to their names on my class roster. This is a way that I can keep track of who is or is not moving forward in their book. As stated earlier, when kids are matched with the right book, there is generally little trouble, but let's be real. They're kids. Some will test the limits. Some just want to see if we are paying attention. If a student is not really reading a text, the page number he or she indentifies aloud in class during a status check will just be whatever happens to roll off his or her tongue. The student won't remember several days later what page number was given, but I will because it is on my chart. It has become a most effective method for me to discover if someone needs a chat with me.

While my penchant for joining discussion groups can be a factor in keeping kids moving forward with their text, during Status of the Class I put another device in place to help keep kids honest. I generally select one or two kids to have a public-private conversation with. Such conversations take place in front of the entire class, but I speak to the student as if it were just the two of us. For example, we are moving around the room at lightning speed with one student after another taking a turn, standing, showing the book, providing all the required information. Danny is just moving into his turn, and when he identifies his book as Neal Shusterman's *Full Tilt*, I suddenly interrupt and begin to gush. "*Full Tilt! Full Tilt!*" I explode with enthusiasm and begin talking only to Danny but with everyone listening. "I loved that book. How exciting that you picked that one. Okay, what page are you on? Well, then you've gotten to the part where the older brother meets Cassandra. What did you think about Shusterman's description of her? How about the setting of when they first met—did that work for you? Where do you think Quinn really is?" If Danny's in second grade instead of seventh, I'm asking the same types of questions about *My Dog, Cat* by Marty Crisp.

I don't want this to come off as an interrogation rather an enthusiastic conversation. The students get a huge kick out of it, and they are always on the edge of their seats wondering who it will be this time. Of course, I haven't read every book they have read, but I have often read a few of the ones they are reading, so I just wait until one comes along that I know. Invariably, they start thinking I've read them all. This is just one more way to encourage kids to make time for reading—and to be honest about whether they are prioritizing reading in their weekly routine. Let's keep in mind that kids' lives are busy just as ours are. We may get them hooked on a book that they are really excited about, but there's still other homework, sports, music, family, and on and on. A little extra incentive to set aside some time to read doesn't hurt, and these status checks are a simple way to achieve that while also providing some other significant benefits.

Student-Delivered Book Chats

I remember supervising a student teacher several years ago with whom I very much enjoyed working. It was clear that she was going to make a fine teacher. I felt that she was very "teachable" and open to constructive criticism and suggestions, but in truth, there had not been a lot of areas where she needed significant assistance. And then I arrived in class one day to find that her students were giving book chats to their peers.

By the end of the second book chat, I was thinking about forcefully jabbing my ballpoint pen into my neck in an effort to sever my jugular. I knew it would be painful but not nearly as painful as what I was watching happening before my eyes. The student teacher was clearly feigning interest—good for her. I knew she was feigning interest because feigned interest was all that was possible. The cooperating teacher was falling asleep—one of those moments where you're fighting with all you've got and losing: your head falls and then your neck snaps back and you realize what just happened and hope no one noticed. I have news for you. Someone has always noticed. Every child in the room, with the exception of the one speaking, was in motion: hunting in desks for things, dropping things on the floor so there would be something to pick up off of the floor, playing footsie with a neighbor, doing the hair of the girl in front, eye-motioning with a friend—you get the picture. Our featured speaker is yammering on and on and on about some character putting on his socks—a completely irrelevant moment in the book. His voice is a mumbly, monotone disaster. He makes no eye contact, has no stage presence. Need I go on? I'm betting some of you have seen it before or perhaps endured it in your own classrooms as you wondered, "Why did I ever assign them to present?"

When I am speaking about the need for us to give book chats to our classes, I frequently have teachers ask me if I am an advocate of students also giving book chats. My answer is always the same: only if they are taught how to do so successfully. This means they need some instruction in oral presentation and a chance to practice those skills before they stand and deliver in the classroom. This also means that a rubric will be used during the evaluation that takes into consideration their oral speaking skills and delivery.

In addition to preparing kids to orally deliver successfully, we have to teach them how to talk about books before telling them to do it. I hate traditional book reports.

Why? Because kids don't learn much by preparing them. Teachers assign book reports in many cases so they have a measure by which to decide whether a student has read a book. A well-written and successfully delivered book chat is a far better measure, and a wider range of skills are put to use as we help students learn to write and deliver such talks.

Figure 6.3 (also in Appendix D) is provided to you with great pride. Of all the rubrics I have created in my career, this is my ultimate, best-ever, most-refined, I-finally-got-it-right rubric. If I had to appear before the great rubric king and present the one rubric I had created that had been the most successful of my career, this is the one that I would bring. I have personally used it in my own classrooms with great success to help students in grades four to eight learn to write and talk about books in interesting ways.

Much of the rubric is self-explanatory, but I encourage you to consider that some of the structures with regard to the characters and plot are desperately needed by kids. For example, they need to learn to make conscious choices about which characters to include and which characters to leave out. Setting minimums or maximums forces choice. Also, I have provided them with some guides in the form of subpoints on the rubric to help them know what might be of interest when introducing a character. Students also need to learn which elements of the plot to include, and they must learn to move from one element to the next expeditiously rather than languishing forever and detailing trivia. The time limit on the presentation as well as the need to include all the required elements force students to begin identifying and cutting extraneous information from their book chats.

I have always believed that being a strategic teacher is the best way to go. What I mean is that I believe there is a right and a wrong time to introduce certain topics, assignments, and so forth. I never ask kids to begin preparing book chats that would be presented to their peers before they have heard me give many, many book chats in class. Though mine might not follow the exact model of this rubric, I am an accomplished public speaker who has advanced beyond the need for such structures. And that is okay for the kids to hear because it is what should happen. As we become more proficient at anything, our need for the crutches we might use when we begin should fade away.

When I decide my students have had enough exposure to my book chats, it becomes their turn to talk. I pass out the rubric with no intention of reviewing it all at once—

FIGURE 6.3

Book Chat Evaluation Rubric

Student's Name _____   Comments

EFFECTIVE HOOK/INTRODUCTION   _____ /04

☐ creative, attention-getter (2)

☐ author and title identified

☐ genre correctly identified

BOOK CLEARLY SHOWN TO AUDIENCE   _____ /02

MAIN CHARACTER(S) INTRODUCED   _____ /12
(LIMIT: THREE)

☐ protagonist/antagonist (as applicable)

☐ age

☐ physical description

☐ personality (general disposition, chief likes/dislikes)

☐ primary goal(s) of character

☐ comparison drawn to a well-known character or real-life person

SUPPORTING CHARACTERS INTRODUCED   _____ /03
(LIMIT: FOUR)

☐ relationship to main character

☐ role in story

☐ additional pertinent information as needed

PLOT DISCUSSED PRECISELY   _____ /14
AND CONCISELY

☐ setting(s)

☐ major problem

☐ complications

☐ climax

☐ resolution

☐ conflict(s)

☐ theme(s)

[Discussion of the plot should move in the order presented here: setting, major problem, complications, climax, etc. Each of these words must be *specifically* stated aloud during the Book Chat. These words must also be in boldface type in the manuscript.]

Book Chat Evaluation Rubric (cont.)

POWERFUL PASSAGE READ ALOUD _____ /07

- ☐ sufficient background provided
- ☐ passage is dramatic/climactic
- ☐ superior oral reading (3)

DELIVERY _____ /12

- ☐ volume
- ☐ rate
- ☐ enunciation/articulation
- ☐ pitch/tone
- ☐ eye contact
- ☐ stage presence

CLOSING _____ /03

- ☐ creative (2)
- ☐ clear closure

MANUSCRIPT _____ /19

- ☐ strong vocabulary (3)
- ☐ clear transitions (3)
- ☐ bold headings with reduced type size as per model (2)
- ☐ cohesive written text (4)
- ☐ strong writing mechanics (4)
- ☐ **APPEARANCE OF MANUSCRIPT (3)**

OVERALL IMPRESSION _____ /20

TIME ALLOCATION MET (8 MIN. MAX) _____ /04

TOTAL _____ /100

GRADE _____

Delivery Start Time _____ : _____

Delivery Stop Time _____ : _____

too much information. They'll be on overload. I give them a few minutes to look it over, then I entertain initial questions for a few minutes. Following that, we move on with whatever is happening in class that day. The next day, I pass out an actual sample of a book chat that was written using the rubric as a guide. I allow students to review the written book chat, and we discuss its merits and weaknesses. We then return to the focus of class for the day. On the third day, we discuss just the hook section of the rubric in depth and compare it quite painstakingly to the sample written book chat I provided the day before. We grade the hook section according to the rubric.

I then model the openings of four book chats for my class; I allow them to review the openings of these book chats in written form before they watch me deliver them. They then work in discussion groups to grade me on each one. Of course, some are terribly written (on purpose) and some terribly delivered (also on purpose). I try to have strengths and weaknesses in each of them for the kids to discover and discuss. When we are done, my students begin to write the openings of their book chats during class time. I try to give them at least twenty minutes of in-class writing time to get a good start. The next day, they will peer-conference their openings using the rubric to help them.

We will follow a similar process for each section of the book chat. I use the rubric as an instructional tool—teaching kids that it can help them learn to write well. I don't overwhelm them by giving them too much at once. Providing them with a completed written book chat to compare to the rubric each day as we examine a section is wonderful; however, I re-collect that sample each day before they begin writing. I don't want them to lean on it too much. Before they write the next section, I continue the practice of having them compare the appropriate section of the rubric to that same section of the sample written book chat. I again model examples from four different book chats and let them discuss and evaluate. When we are on the minor character section of the rubric, for example, I will pass out four totally different minor character sections from four different book chats. Some will be poorly written, some a little better, and I will deliver them with all different levels of flair, just as I did with the introductory section of the book chat. Again, they will evaluate via discussion with their peers. All of this happens before they write their minor character section.

I am hoping you can see a huge difference between what I am describing here and what a teacher does who just assigns kids to write and deliver a book report or passes out a rubric and says, "Use this as a guide to write a book chat." The difference, of course, is that I am *teaching* kids to write the book chats—scaffolding them every step of the way. I am not overwhelming them with the entire thing at once, and I am not sending it home so their parents can have some homework to complete for my class. When the time comes to actually deliver these book chats, the kids are actually excited to hear one another because they know the level of work that went into them; we did it together in our classroom for the most part. And although I know they are far more interested and well rehearsed than my student teacher's kids of so long ago, I still know enough not to schedule more than four per day. No matter how good they might be, they're not accomplished speakers. Subjecting the entire class to lengthy stretches of time listening to these is too much, and attention will wane, resulting in an audience that is less engaged for students who speak near the end. That is not productive, not fair, and not fun.

FROM THE TRENCHES

Several years ago I received a phone call from a parent I had not heard from in several years. I had taught her son as a sixth grader and enjoyed him very much. As we spoke, I quickly did the math, realized he would be in eleventh grade by now and that I was five years older, and resisted the urge to hang up rather than be faced with inevitable comments on how time has flown.

Mrs. (I'll leave out her name, just like Junie B. Jones does for her teacher) wanted to schedule an appointment with me. I couldn't imagine why, but readily agreed because she had never been one to fear. Mrs. arrived on time a few days later with brownies from Kirschbaum's bakery in Western Springs, Illinois, which is what you bring when you visit me and want to make me exceedingly happy. To my great surprise, she had scheduled her appointment simply to thank me!

She told me that her son, my former student, was now in eleventh-grade (see, I knew it would come up) honors-level English and that he had just completed one of his biggest assignments of the year, which was to prepare and deliver an oral overview of a classic text. She smiled, "Dr. Layne, Billy was the only student in the class to receive an A. The teacher wrote a tremendously encouraging note on his paper and said that it was the best-written and best-delivered assignment she'd seen in her twenty-seven years of teaching." I smiled in response and told her I was delighted to hear the news. She then looked me square in the eye and said, "I've always been realistic about Billy's work, Dr. Layne. He's a good solid student with some high and low points each year in all of his classes. He is not the caliber of student who would typically receive this type of accolade . . . and to be the only one in the class!" I responded that sometimes they surprise us, but her facial expression told me she wasn't buying that explanation, and then her voice took on a bit of an official tone. "Dr. Layne, I asked Billy how he was able to earn such a tremendous mark on this assignment, and he shrugged casually like it was really no big deal and said, 'Mom, all I did was do everything Dr. Layne taught me in sixth grade.'" She said he walked over to his desk, opened a drawer, pulled out a piece of paper and handed it to her with a sly grin as he said, "I saved his book chat rubric, Mom. There are some things you just know better than to ever throw away. I'm taking this thing with me when I go to college!"

Never underestimate the power of our first teachers—our parents—to ignite the passion for books. The environment in which we are raised and our early role models *must* be given the responsibility and credit they deserve.

I was very fortunate to have the parents I had. My dad was a Ph.D. reading specialist, so books and education were held in high regard in our home. I have fond memories of my mom, reading from Mother Goose, and the whimsical, rhythmical verses of Ogden Nash and Dr. Seuss. My dad's special talent was changing his voice to capture the intriguing dialect of James Whitcomb Riley. We didn't always have TV, so we checked out books at the library and listened to stories on our record player.

When I started school, my teachers recognized and further encouraged my passion for the written word. My kindergarten teacher didn't get angry when I wrote my favorite word,

 *antidisestablishmentarianism*, on the blackboard during nap time. My first-grade teacher invited me to read one of my stories in front of the PTA. It was about Sally, a little girl who painted herself and her dog with red lipstick. I'll never forget the jittery joy of that moment. And finally, my second-grade teacher, when I turned in a story entitled "The Man Without a Head," graciously resisted reporting me to authorities. Instead, she wrote at the top of my paper: "Karen, what an imagination! This is quite a story!" Although now yellowed and slightly tattered, I still have it. These three teachers, by their wisdom, nurtured in me the courage to believe in my ability to successfully use the written word. Today, as a children's author, it is my hope and deepest desire that my words serve to ignite in children the flame of passion for reading.

—Karen Beaumont

CHAPTER 7

Nothing's More Dangerous Than a Teacher with a Good Idea: Igniting a Passion by Opening a Reading Lounge

I struggle to believe there was ever a new teacher with more enthusiasm than me. Maybe some have been *as* enthusiastic, but *more* enthusiastic would be a hard sell to anyone who knew me then. I could not wait to have my own classroom, and I wanted everything to be as authentic as possible. For example, I refused to use pre-cut letters for bulletin boards. No sir, none of those store-bought letters for me. My letters were traced from old-fashioned patterns I borrowed from a teacher friend—these letters weren't like anything they sold in the teacher stores, either. I look back and laugh at the time I spent on such things when I should have been poring over the curriculum! It's difficult, though, to make sound decisions when you are young, inexperienced, and blinded by enthusiasm for a job you only *think* you understand.

I was terrifically excited, as I began setting up that first classroom, to have "Mr. Layne's Reading Corner." I made a great, flashy sign (the letters were hand-drawn and cut, of course) and hung it from the ceiling. I bought a chair with a nice back for me, and two special seats for the kids. One was a blue beanbag chair and the other was a giant purple pillow. I could hardly contain myself as I surveyed the reading utopia I had created. I slept for weeks with visions of the first time I would invite the students to join me in Mr. Layne's Reading Corner!

The day finally came, and I could sense the excitement as I gave the first students of my career a tour of my classroom. I admit to lingering a bit longer in the area near the reading corner. No need to rush by and have them fail to catch the wave of excitement I had planned to generate. Much to my relief, when the fateful hour arrived and I sounded the call to meet me in the reading corner, there was tremendous excitement as they scrambled from their desks.

I remember the feeling of contentment that washed over me as I turned to look at what I had created—and then stood gasping for air as the beans flew from the blue beanbag and the stuffing came loose from the purple pillow. Chaos was raining down on my first day of teaching! There was pulling and shoving and screaming and crying as twenty-four fifth graders all tried to get either the beanbag, the pillow, or both. A fleeting thought—they never told us about this in our methods classes— and then I was forced to impersonate an action hero.

Necessity compelled me to throw my body into the fray while shouting that I had a system (made up at that exact moment) for managing the beanbag chair and the pillow, and if everyone would just calm down and listen I would tell them all about it. I proceeded to craft "passes" from index cards, draw a blue circle on one and a purple square on the other, and assign each of these magnificent seats to the two names drawn from my hat. "You see there, children," I explained. "Now we know who has the blue beanbag and who has the purple pillow for this entire week, and there's no reason for anymore of this insanity." And then a sweet young thing spoke words now immortalized in my mind. "Teacher, may we share?" My naïve response to that question and the ensuing events led to more casualties than the Civil War, but that's a story for another time. The point of all of this is to say that environment matters—it matters a lot.

Over the years, I struggled to build Mr. Layne's Reading Corner into something bigger and better each year. Why? Primarily because of the response I was getting. Kids wanted to get out of those desks and *be* with books. Maybe I was reading aloud, maybe they were reading silently, maybe they were reading to each other—it didn't matter. What mattered was that we were away from the desks. I had read articles in plenty of journals and seen other professional materials that reminded me that environment matters and that the opportunity for kids to get up from desks is important. Who among us looks for the most uncomfortable chair in the house when we want to enjoy some great text? Over the years of my own classroom experience, I came to understand just how powerful it can be for students to have a comfortable space to be with text. That realization—and some issues with technology—led me to form a team of teaching colleagues who created a reading lounge in our school.

The Reading Lounge

How many technology labs are in your building? Do the computers ever all work when you go there? I believe there is a conspiracy against teachers; if you take twenty-two students to a computer lab that contains thirty computers, at least nine will not be functioning, leaving you with one student who has to share. When kids are working on individual projects, this presents a difficulty.

In my dream school, the computer labs all have seven more computers than the largest class size in the building, allowing for a large number of computers to be broken when a teacher arrives with his or her class. At one point in my career, I joined the growing number of teachers who boycott labs where the equipment doesn't function. After all, we're supposed to be protecting our instructional time! A good way to do that is to avoid dragging everyone through the halls to a lab where the equipment consistently fails to function as needed. Instead, let's stay in the classroom and hand-write persuasive pieces on why we should have equipment that works in a school.

Several years ago, I was sitting in a faculty meeting when our leader mentioned that there was talk of adding another computer lab to our building. I quickly put on my poker face, but my mind was racing with thoughts that were mutinous at the very least. We already had one lab that you couldn't count on to work. Now we would have two! And they would both house computers with totally different operating systems, just to further ensure that any potential for educational progress (such as having enough working computers for every student to complete an assignment) was thwarted.

I became quite fired up about the issue and, with the help of my wily and wise comrades in the language arts department, began advocating for a reading lounge instead of, or in addition to, another technology lab. Our classrooms were pretty cramped with big desks for big junior high bodies; creating space to get away from desks within the classroom was a struggle. Our feeling was that if there was enough room in our building for another computer lab, there ought to be enough room to create a space for kids to enjoy being with text! And thus the idea for a reading lounge was born: in large part out of frustration over technology issues. Who says the technological revolution is hurting reading? In this case, I couldn't disagree more!

For those of you working in an elementary school building and who panicked when you read, "language arts department" in the preceding paragraphs, don't worry. Just last year I was invited to "cut the ribbon" on the opening of a reading lounge at an elementary school building in Indiana. Reading lounges are not just for junior high and middle schools. They belong in any building where part of the instructional goal is to create lifetime readers.

A LOUNGE, NOT THE LIBRARY

I have served as a resource for teachers in many U.S. states where educators have heard me speak and resolved to open reading lounges in their own buildings. One of the first questions I always hear is, "Couldn't we just use the library?" My answer is clear: No. The library of any school should be a dynamic hub of activity at all times and much of the time should be available to the entire school. My friend Jeanne Dawson at Victory Lakes Intermediate School in League City, Texas, knows all about what a library should be like, and as far as I'm concerned she is the go-to person for creating libraries that live. Reading lounges do not belong in libraries because the lounges need to be easily accessible for classroom teachers to reserve for read-aloud time and SSR (or whatever you call it). If a lounge is being used the way it should be, it would become clear that it could not be in the library because people would constantly be asking the librarian to "close the library so my class and I can read and discuss this book."

In my dream school, the reading lounge has two doors. One door leads to the hallway; this is the door classes use to enter and exit the reading lounge. The second door connects the lounge directly to the library and all that great reading material. This door is used by individuals who are moving back and forth between the reading lounge and the library when returning or getting new reading material. We do not drag entire classrooms in and out of this doorway on a regular basis because we remain respectful of the fact that other groups may be in the library at any given time; the distraction of a freeway between the library and the lounge might not be appreciated.

READING LOUNGE ROADBLOCKS

My suggestion to faculty who want to make a reading lounge their mission would be to form a RELODIT (Reading Lounge or Die Trying) Committee. These endeavors are not for the faint of heart. You *will* meet roadblocks. You will run into naysayers. Whenever you are trying to do something new and innovative that is terrifically good for kids, you can be sure if you are in the field of education that you will hear comments like, "We tried something like that back in '59. It didn't work." I have generated this response to such militant personalities: "Well, Elinor, since they were still churning butter back when you tried something like this, perhaps we might give it another look-see. How about that?" I've never cared for bullies, and we're crazy if we think the only bullies in schools are wearing backpacks. Some of them are wearing school-bus earrings and should have retired twenty-seven years ago.

One common roadblock is being told that there is no space for a reading lounge because there aren't empty classrooms in the building that are unused. As the title of this chapter indicates, passionate teachers with great ideas do not give up. Instead, they find a way around. I have heard stories of reading lounges on stages, in board rooms (Why does the school board need a huge room dedicated to their meetings once or twice a month that sits empty the rest of the year? They should be the first in line to sit in folding chairs at card tables to make space for kids to have an improved experience in school!), in mobile classrooms, in converted garages, and even in classrooms that were made empty through innovative scheduling. Yes, space is an obvious issue that must be addressed, but that's why you have a big committee. More minds equal more possible solutions to hurdles.

Another common obstacle in education is: there's no money. Yes, there is too money! I have never, in any job I have had, believed anyone who told me there was no money. It simply is not true. Yes, there is money. There is always money. The question is how it is being allocated and who controls it. I look at every person in authority as someone who either has access to discretionary funds or has access to someone else who has access to discretionary funds. You have to ask yourself, if the reading lounge were the principal's passion, the superintendent's passion, the president of the school board's passion . . . would there be money? Would a way be made? The answer, and we all know it, is YES.

Now, in most cases, we are not talking about huge amounts of money when compared with what is paid to equip technology labs or to sponsor athletic programs. In fact, the first reading lounge we had at Butler Junior High in Oak Brook, Illinois, was furnished in beanbag chairs, big pillows, and video rockers from Target for a few hundred dollars provided by the PTA. True, we had to purchase all the furniture again every year for three years, not because the kids were abusing it, but because a $19.00 beanbag is not made to hold up against the major use it receives at school multiple periods a day for an entire year. Midway through year three, we realized that the Target furniture was not meeting our needs.

At this time in history, Sears had a series of nationwide furniture stores called Sears Homelife. A store opened quite close to our school, and we language arts teachers simply *had* to visit. It was the neighborly thing to do. Needless to say, when we left we had furniture and fabric selected, a huge discount on the order, and no tax. If only we could get $9,000 to pay the bill. Well, there's always the PTA or grants we could apply for (foundations love to give grants to people who are doing something innovative, and literacy is always a big cause). There's the principal's secret money fund, the librarian's book-fair profits, the language arts budget, and local businesses who might want their names on a plaque hung outside the room. I'm simply saying that there IS money. Within a few months, we had ours and the furniture was ordered. Our reading lounge, after three years of Target furniture, was going to look and feel like a family room!

The third roadblock is one you might not have to deal with, but I want you to be prepared. As many readers are aware, much of the furniture in a school comes from school furniture catalogs rather than a furniture store. The reason is because all furnishings from those catalogs are flame retardant. From the very start of our venture to turn the lounge into more of a family room, we were committed to avoiding that catalog furniture because it just isn't comfortable. The trouble, of course, became how to make sure the furniture from Sears would be flame retardant. Here is what I discovered: There are companies in the yellow pages that can send people to your school who will spray the furniture to make it flame retardant, and this is what we did at Butler Junior High. We got a certificate to provide to the fire marshal showing that we had done due diligence with regard to this issue. I have since learned that you can buy flame retardant material in a spray can from a hardware store, and do it yourself!

The furniture I am describing and that is pictured in photos on some of these pages (see Figure 7.1) was purchased for our school in 1994 and is still functioning as of the printing of this book. A colleague still working in the building reports that there has been virtually no significant cost in maintaining the furnishings over the past fourteen years. I'd say that's a pretty sound investment.

PROMOTION AND USE OF THE READING LOUNGE

Once you have space allocated for your lounge and some type of furnishings for it (remember, we didn't start with the snazzy furniture! It was three years of Target beanbags), you need to promote this new space and allow every class in the building

FIGURE 7.1

READING LOUNGE AT BUTLER JUNIOR HIGH IN OAK BROOK, ILLINOIS

access to it. We used a simple three-ring binder with a calendar that listed each day of the school year and each period of the day. This way any teacher in the building could schedule, well in advance, a day or period they intended to use the lounge. The binder may be kept in the faculty lounge, in the main office, or in the reading lounge itself—wherever you feel it will be most easily accessible and work best for your building. In an elementary school building, where specific periods may not be designated, you can split the day into half-hour slots or whatever you deem appropriate.

It's no secret that some teachers need more scaffolding than others when a new idea comes to school. One of the ways we tried to promote the reading lounge for everyone was to use faculty meetings to suggest ways teachers of many different disciplines might make use of it. Lo and behold, several teachers began taking advantage of it! The Spanish teacher took her students to the lounge to read to them in Spanish and then explained an upcoming reading assignment. The social studies teacher took her students to the lounge following a library trip where they each selected a book related to World War II. They began reading these World War II books for her annual class project in the reading lounge! We drew the name of one study hall teacher each week and that teacher was allowed to use the lounge for study hall that week—but no doing homework in there! The reading lounge is for reading.

I have supplied the rules we put in place for the reading lounge in Figure 7.2, in case some of these spur your own ideas. We did not want the furniture destroyed with pens, pencils, and other items sticking out of back pockets, and we saw no reason to allow writing utensils in the lounge. It was created for reading, not for written work. We felt sure that if we gave the kids an inch, they'd take a mile, so we made it clear from the beginning that the lounge was not going to become a glorified homework room. We stalled Olympic events in the lounge by having the rule that an adult enters before the kids. Amazingly, the furniture does not lend itself to trampoline exercises nearly as frequently when this rule is in place. Kids were not allowed in the lounge without an adult present. Someone who is willing to open and monitor the lounge before school, during the lunch period (for the time after the kids are finished eating), or after school for awhile offers a wonderful way to allow more reading to take place. Perhaps a rotating schedule of volunteers made up of faculty, staff, and parents could make this a reality.

FIGURE 7.2

READING LOUNGE GUIDELINES

The reading lounge is open to all classes in our school. A binder containing sign-out information is located in the school office, and teachers may sign up to bring their classes to the lounge for any period of the day. Please follow the guidelines below so that the lounge remains in good condition for future use by all groups of students.

- Adult supervision is required for the lounge to be open.
- Please do not take food, sharp objects, or writing utensils inside the lounge.
- Shoes on footrests only.
- Please turn off lamps prior to leaving the lounge.
- Please do not move furniture in the lounge.

DECORATING THE READING LOUNGE

The décor of the reading lounge is also worth considering. When it comes to buying the furniture, of course, we had a color scheme that went with the carpet in the room. We also worked to get several pieces of leather or vinyl furniture that would be easy to keep clean and looking nice (Figure 7.3).

We purchased a few end tables as well as lamps for both the floor and the tables. The overhead fluorescent lights were basically banned by the kids in no time. They preferred the natural light from the windows in the room and lights from our lamps!

It goes without saying that the decorating in the lounge should promote reading. One of our best decisions, I believe, was to sponsor an annual poster contest to advertise reading and the use of the lounge. Each year, the winner received a $50.00 gift certificate to a bookstore, and his or her winning poster was matted, framed, and hung in the lounge. A small plaque was attached to designate the winner's name and the year. As you can see in Figure 7.4, this became a fine way to add to the feel of the lounge. Figure 7.5 includes the rules developed for our Reading Lounge Poster Contest.

I have often been asked about books in the reading lounge—as in, Did we have any in there? The answer is, yes. We all donated tons of great reads from our classroom libraries. We decided not to put a checkout system in place because it would be too cumbersome. While kids took books from the lounge from time to time, the

FIGURE 7.3

READING LOUNGE AT THE PRAIRIE HILL SCHOOL IN CARY, ILLINOIS

library was a mainstay of the reading program and, with teachers using many of the strategies discussed in this text, our kids were rarely without a book. They usually already had a plan for the next book they were going to read, and finding it in the library was much faster than hunting for it in the reading lounge, where there was no particular system for shelving materials.

When we reached the point where we had the lounge furnished with truly nice furniture provided, in large part, by the generosity of the PTA, we decided that something should be done to ensure the longevity of the lounge. Having a PTA representative working closely with us was something we requested, and as luck would have it, we had a lovely woman, who truly cared about literacy, jump on the bandwagon.

There was a large bulletin-board space right outside the lounge door, and we suggested having a mural done that would designate the space as the school read-

FIGURE 7.4

READING LOUNGE POSTER CONTEST WINNERS ON DISPLAY

FIGURE 7.5

READING LOUNGE POSTER CONTEST

We are looking for a poster that promotes READING! Can *you* design it for us? Stop in the Reading Lounge to check out winning entries from previous years.

ENTRY REQUIREMENTS:

- The poster needs to be more visual than verbal. Very few words!
- Paper must be white and 18 x 24 inches.
- No three-dimensional materials may be used.
- Media options include pencils, crayons, chalk, paint, markers, torn paper . . .
- The poster must be designed individually.
- The poster may be *vertical* or *horizontal.* Consider both options!
- A one-inch border of empty white space is necessary all the way around.
- Artwork must be original—no famous characters, copies of book covers, etc.
- Write your name legibly in pencil on the *back side* of the poster.

– POSTER DUE DATE IS _____.

ENTRIES THAT DO NOT ADHERE TO THE REQUIREMENTS ABOVE WILL BE DISQUALIFIED.

THE WINNING POSTER WILL BE MATTED, FRAMED, AND PERMANENTLY ON DISPLAY IN THE READING LOUNGE. A NAME PLAQUE

WILL BE ADDED TO THE WINNING POSTER, AND THE WINNER WILL RECEIVE A $50.00 GIFT CERTIFICATE TO A LOCAL BOOKSTORE.

---

ing lounge, stating that it was "created and supported" by the school PTA. Students submitted their designs for the mural with the understanding that a professional artist would be hired to translate the winning design to a mural. What excitement! Figure 7.6 shows the mural that now stands outside the door to the reading lounge. Over the years, the wonderful relationship we had with the PTA led to the addition to the room of a ceiling fan, vertical blinds, and several blankets with the school logo on them. (Figure 7.7 shows a reading lounge with several seating options and a school blanket.) The PTA even took responsibility for having the blankets cleaned each quarter of the year and returning them to the lounge. What a blessing to witness and be part of a partnership that benefits every child in the school!

FIGURE 7.6

SCHOOL READING LOUNGE MURAL

FIGURE 7.7

READING LOUNGE AT CEDAR CREST INTERMEDIATE SCHOOL IN HUNTINGBURG, INDIANA

FROM THE TRENCHES

It makes me laugh that society seems to want teachers to go to their graves claiming that they did not have favorite students. What are we, superhuman? I will proclaim loud and long that I had favorite colleagues, favorite bosses, and, yes, favorite students. Now, I can comfortably say that I never *favored* certain students. I felt it would be unprofessional to allow anyone to guess by my speech or actions that I had favorite students.

But how can I say that Jori Carqueville was not one of my favorite students? I taught her in fifth grade in 1999 and just had dinner with her in Chicago last year. She has sat on the couch in my home and visited many times over the years. She has met my children and my wife. We have laughed and cried together. I named a character in one of my young adult novels after her. She has my cell phone number; I have hers. And I'm supposed to say I never had any favorite students? I could add several other names to the list from the fifteen years of my public school career, and the list could become longer if I included all the college and university students I have taught at four institutions over ten years.

That background is needed so that I can talk about Ryan McNamara—a fabulous young man who maintained contact with me even when I was no longer his teacher. Ryan and I met for lunch one summer prior to his sophomore year of high school. I had heard from him occasionally during his freshman year, but this lunch was the first face-to-face catch-up on things. I came away from that lunch thinking Ryan should someday run the government. Maybe then I could have hope for the future.

We had been talking about books read in high school, and he put his sandwich down and spoke in a rather disgusted tone. "Dr. Layne, they don't care about reading in high school." I was shocked. I knew several of the high school teachers and had very high opinions of them. I was forced to defend.

"Ryan, that just isn't true. I know a lot of the high school teachers, and they love books! Why would you say something like that?"

"Well, we don't have a reading lounge! I asked, and

they said there's no space" he fired back, and I began to laugh. I tried to explain the reading lounge "wave" hadn't quite taken the nation by storm yet and that perhaps he should not use that as the determining factor in whether a school cared about reading. And that is when, in my mind, his presidential bid began.

Ryan was thoughtful for a moment, and then he asked me an important question. "Dr. Layne, did they have computers back when you were in school?" (Did I really say this kid was a favorite of mine?) I grinned. "No, Ryan, they did not have computers that long ago. We had just retired the horses and the buggies when I was in high school." He took a moment to give me a quick "sorry" before launching into his main point.

"Okay, so then having computers in the schools is a relatively new thing—maybe in the last twenty years or so, right?"

"I could agree with you on that. Yes, that's probably close to true." I had no idea where he was going with this.

"So, if computers are pretty new to the school, then so are computer labs."

"Right."

"So, Dr. Layne, where'd they get all the *space* for these computer labs? I mean every school in America or in the whole world didn't suddenly build an addition to house computer labs, but nearly every school you walk into has a computer lab. So I'm asking you, where'd they find the space for these labs?"

I was dumbfounded. "Ryan, that's a very good point. I guess I never really thought about it that way before."

"Dr. Layne, I think they made space; they found space because they decided it was important. If reading was important at the high school, they wouldn't be telling me they didn't have space for a reading lounge."

At that moment, I told Ryan McNamara that I thought he should one day become president of the United States. I haven't changed my mind.

Ah, Mrs. Rouse—soft-spoken, smile-lined, story-loving Mrs. Rouse! Her fourth-grade classroom overflowed with reading material—picture books, chapter books, novels, biographies, Archie comics, encyclopedias, back issues of *Highlights for Children*, atlases, poetry anthologies, travel pamphlets, and the morning newspaper. It was a miraculous hodgepodge of the printed word—a world unlike any I'd ever entered before.

Mrs. Rouse eschewed those deathly, dull, reading textbooks used in the other classrooms and instead expected each of her students to choose a book from a special shelf labeled "Mrs. R. Recommends." Choosing was always difficult for me. I'd stand in front of the titles in a fevered state of indecision. Should I tackle an adventure like *Island of the Blue Dolphins*? Laugh my pants off with *Homer Price*? Go back in time with *The Witch of Blackbird Pond*? Often, Mrs. Rouse made the choice for me. "This is one of my favorite books," she'd say, handing me a copy of *Misty of Chincoteague* or *Anne of Green Gables*. I'd take the book and press it to my heart. If Mrs. Rouse loved it, I knew I would, too.

After reading the book, I would sit down with Mrs. Rouse to discuss it. "What did you like about the story?" she would ask. "Was there anything you didn't like about the story? Why, or why not?" Then she'd listen, carefully and uncritically, while I talked about the story's merits (or demerits after being scared silly by *Jane-Emily*). What a heady, exhilarating experience! Looking back on it now, I realize we were actually discussing plot and character and theme. But at the time, I simply drew pleasure from "talking books" with someone who took my literary opinions seriously.

Then, of course, there was story time. Every day after lunch recess, Mrs. Rouse would read aloud, transporting us to the Metropolitan Museum of Art with those mixed-up files kids, or

through the wardrobe with those curious British kids. She always seemed to stop at the most exciting parts.

"One more chapter," we'd beg.

Mrs. Rouse looked at us, her eyes twinkling. "Well," she'd finally say. "I guess fractions can wait another fifteen minutes." Oh, yes, she knew what she was doing, that crafty teacher. She was hooking us on stories, turning us into lifelong reading addicts. And it worked!

Not long ago, I bumped into an old school friend who told me the sad news of Mrs. Rouse's passing.

"She turned me into a reader," he said.

"She turned *me* into a children's author," I said.

I think, in tribute, I'll reread *Homer Price*.

—Candace Fleming

CHAPTER 8

There's a Party Goin' on Right Here: Igniting a Passion by Celebrating Books

Everybody likes to go to a party, but reluctant readers rarely like to go to school—not much of a party atmosphere, in their opinion. I'm not saying everything about school needs to be enjoyable or that there aren't some things we just need to pony up and learn whether we think it's going to lead to a good time or not. I've never subscribed to the belief that school needs to be the ultimate good-time hangout, but as I mentioned in Chapter 4, there's not much about school that *is* enjoyable for kids who don't do "the reading thing."

A major goal throughout my career has been to provide opportunities for my students to engage with text through activities that generate some excitement about reading. What's wrong with a little bit of a party atmosphere now and then if kids end up engaged with text? The strategies, activities, and suggestions spread throughout this chapter come not only from my own innovations but also from the experiences and wise counsel of colleagues in classrooms around the world. I have found them to be tremendously motivating and extremely effective in working with kids at a myriad of grade levels, and as most of you know, with some minor (or sometimes major) tweaking, nearly every great idea can work for every grade level.

Golden Recommendation Shelf

I have been talking about it for years. Finally, I get to write about it. The cheap $3.97 shelf I bought at an unfinished furniture store was the harbinger of a classroom transformation. After getting the shelf hung in the classroom (Dunkin' Donuts make for happy custodians) but leaving it empty, I had students who were giving

Curious George a run for his money. When my students returned on day two, they found the shelf was still empty but now it was sparkly gold in color, and I remained infuriatingly silent. Day three brought the addition of a sign above the shelf that read, "The Golden Recommendation Shelf," but still the shelf was vacant of any type of material. By the fourth day, I was keenly aware that I could have put anything at all on that shelf (dog food, used pens, plastic silverware, dirty socks), and the kids would have been thrilled. They just needed something to be there. Of course, on day four there *was* finally something there—books!

I began by placing nine of my favorite books for fifth graders on the shelf. When they heard that these were my favorites, everyone wanted to check them out. The interest level in those titles was off the charts for everyone in the classroom, and in a matter of moments, the shelf was empty. I was thrilled it had worked so well; I was sad the shelf was already empty. I returned home resolved to restock this exciting new space. Next up, my autographed books were added. Of course, the students jumped to wild and inane conclusions when they saw that a book had been autographed personally to me by these authors (no, Ben, a book signed by Barbara Park does not mean I have had dinner with her on her yacht! Does Barbara Park even have a yacht?). But again, that shelf moved merchandise! Over time, it became the golden recommendation bookcase because the shelf couldn't hold all the great books I wanted to feature (Figure 8.1). Figure 8.2 includes some of my best suggestions for making a golden shelf (or bookcase) work for you. Keep in mind that you can call it anything you want. "Mrs. B's Purple Treasure Shelf" is going to be just as effective. The idea is that we are drawing kids' attention to books through the use of a tool that highlights certain titles.

First Read Club

I think it's clear that I am a big advocate for classroom teacher and school librarian collaboration. Here's an opportunity to continue working toward that goal. Most school libraries add to the book collection at designated times throughout the year. For example, a librarian might get new books in at the beginning of each quarter of the school year. If so, how about a teacher and the librarian sponsoring a club—The First Read Club—where members are invited to the library to preview the new books (once they are cataloged and ready for checkout) and select one to check out

FIGURE 8.1

THE GOLDEN RECOMMENDATION BOOKCASE

FIGURE 8.2

THE GOLDEN RECOMMENDATION SHELF/BOOKCASE

SUGGESTIONS FOR ADDED EXCITEMENT!

1. Write a personal note inside each book explaining to the students why you have placed it on the shelf.

2. Record the amount of *time* you waited to have each autographed book signed. If it was a lot of time, explain all that you "gave up" to get it signed so the students know how important they are.

3. Take a photo of yourself with the author and tape it inside the book.

4. Buy hardcover books for this shelf whenever possible.

5. Have a special sign-out log for these titles.

6. Stock multiple titles by favorite authors to give kids the idea that if they like one book by an author, they might like more!

7. Keep some of your favorite books from childhood on this shelf.

8. If a friend gives you a book that is meaningful, have it inscribed and place it on the shelf so kids see that books make great gifts!

---

and read prior to the books being made available schoolwide? As kids complete their books, they report in either to the teacher or to the librarian, not so much to prove that the book was read but to discuss how they liked it, identify other kids who might like it, and so forth. At the conclusion of this chat, a sticker or label is placed in the book that reads, "This book was first read by _____." I have seen more kids' faces light up with excitement to see their names written on those labels—you'd think they had just won an Academy Award! Figure 8.3 (also in Appendix D) shows a sticker created by our technology guru and printed on very cheap blank labels from the local office supply store. Reluctant readers, in particular, will love to have their names in these books because they don't typically view themselves as readers, and they are well aware that others do not think of them as readers, either. While it may take more work to get reluctant readers to join the club, once they do, they are typically hooked.

This is not a time-consuming suggestion nor is it going to be terribly hard to implement. You can advertise via posters, school announcements, and the personal touch—both the teacher and the librarian target a few kids, including some reluctant readers, whom they personally invite to join. Many of you reading this book buy trade books for your own classroom several times a year, and some of you get free titles through book club bonus points. Keep in mind that you could start a First Read Club right in your classroom by releasing ten new titles (or whatever number you choose) into the classroom at the beginning of each quarter or semester. You can use the same labels mentioned earlier as well.

FIGURE 8.3

FIRST READ CLUB STICKER

Read Arounds

In Chapter 5, I discussed the previewing of books in great detail; previewing will be a necessary skill for your students to possess in order to successfully engage in what I have always referred to as a read around. I have heard about, read about, and seen this procedure or a variation of it called by many different names, but let's not get hung up on such issues. The point is that it works brilliantly with kids. A Read Around is a wonderful way to allow kids to have access to multiple titles quickly—a fast way to generate interest in text.

I love the idea of building a future reading list with our students. In my dream school (here we go again), every student has a list of titles he or she is hoping to read. We don't have students in this school who enter the library with no idea of what they want to read. Instead, we have students hoping that one of the titles they want to check out is actually on the shelf. The Read Around offers one more opportunity to help build that someday list.

To begin, place a hardcover book on each student's desk. I generally do this before they arrive in the morning, while they are at lunch, during a passing period—sometime when I don't need to use up any instructional time. Why a hardcover book? Because I want that book jacket and all the wonderful information it contains to be available during the preview. The elimination of the book jacket is the primary reason I dislike paperback books. A lot of the great information I have taught kids to tap into during a preview is missing on a paperback book, but on a hardcover it is plentiful.

Next, I remind students of the importance of the preview and ask them to reiterate the kinds of things we consider about the text during a preview. Then I tell students that they will be given approximately one minute and thirty seconds to preview the book on their desks. When I say "pass," everyone who *wants* to passes their book to the next person. Students may elect to keep the book they have at their desk and pass it the next time . . . or they may hold on to their book again! They may choose to "hold" up to three times before they *must* pass the book on to the next person. Of course, when William holds a book and refuses to pass it to Karen, the book that Daniel is passing to William must now be relinquished to Karen. In other words, if William wants to keep what he's got, Karen has to be given William's new offering, which he now won't get to spend any time with at all. The cognitive conflict is delicious!

Some of you have already realized how absolutely necessary the "practice passing" of invisible books will be prior to trying this with real books. I can offer personal testimony to the nightmare that can develop when every student does not know quite specifically to whom he or she is passing his or her book. Students seated in rows have it a bit easier than those whose desks are clustered; however, it takes clear direction from the teacher and practice in advance no matter how kids are seated. It might be obvious that having little ones (K–1) sit on the rug in a circle for their Read Around can eliminate a lengthy stay in a psychiatric ward for the teacher.

Your job is to call "time" and to facilitate the passing of books at the end of rows, when a traffic jam occurs, and so on. You may start everyone out with a minute and thirty seconds on the first book, then call "pass," and give them three minutes on the second book before calling "pass" again and allowing only forty seconds on the third book. Constantly varying the amount of time keeps things hopping. Sometimes, due to the overall length of your entire Read Around (which can be any amount of time you choose) and because of kids' holding certain books, students may get a title back that they've already seen. In such cases, have a few extra books in your hand to trade out. It is not uncommon for kids to assume that if someone passes them a title they have read before, you will swap that book out. I recommend heading this situation off before it happens by explaining that you will do no such thing. How can students who watch the same movies and television shows over and over and who race home to play the same video games night after night legitimately be concerned that they are about to spend ninety seconds with a book they read once before? Kids need to learn that a book can be enjoyed more than once just like other forms of entertainment.

I don't really like kids to take time to write down titles, authors, and such during the Read Around because it wastes too much of their previewing time. To avoid this becoming a concern, I tell them that at the conclusion of the Read Around I will give everyone time to walk the room and record on their Someday Book List or Books to Consider sheet (see Chapter 5) any titles they might be interested in reading.

Elementary/YA Café

A wonderful idea came my way many years ago as I listened to an award-winning high school teacher discuss a "Café" program she put in place that seemed to foster an interest in reading with her high school population. I saw no reason it couldn't work in elementary and middle school; I began tweaking her vision to meet my needs (just as all of you will do with the ideas shared in this book) and found that both reading success and good times with books were available to readers of all levels through her Café idea.

In order for the Café to be effective, there will need to be buy-in from the PTA, an art teacher or artsy-type person or club, the school librarian, and approximately nine faculty or staff members in the building. The Café will meet one morning each month before school for a period lasting between forty and sixty minutes depending on the grade level hosted and book featured. There obviously needs to be time for kids to get into the room, get coats, backpacks, and other items put away, and get some refreshments. During the remaining time a faculty or staff member from the building will introduce a favorite book, explain why it is a favorite, read aloud a long-and-strong excerpt from the book, and answer questions about the book.

The PTA's role is quite simple. They agree to provide hot chocolate and donuts for the Café, which will meet only one morning each month. The school librarian's role is to have several copies of the featured book cataloged and available for check-out on the day the Café meets. The artistically gifted person/people will design some ultra-cool posters that will feature a large photo of each month's reader and a large picture of the book cover of his or her featured book. It is important to create several posters so that the publicity can be strong. Also, the posters should be made so that the book covers and faculty/staff photos can be changed out each month and the posters reused.

One volunteer reader per month from the faculty and staff is key, but you can also get creative. How about the principal's mother as a guest in the Café one month? I recommend a "direct ask" for the first two people featured in the Café. In other words, select two people in the building who are intensely popular and coerce them to agree so that you can start strong. Others can volunteer to fill the slots for the seven remaining months.

It is important to remind the people being featured in the Café that their book needs to be appropriate for the audience. In a middle school, for example, it could easily be that all books featured are appropriate for all grades every month; however, it could also be true that one of your guests selects something that is more appropriate for eighth graders than sixth or seventh graders. In that case, you could have some type of special logo to add to the posters that reads: "This month for eighth grade only!" At the elementary level, you could run the Café for a different grade level each month or for primary only or intermediate only. Obviously, there are many ways to organize the program to best meet the needs of your building and your population. Also, remind staff and faculty that if someone really wants to participate but doesn't have a book in mind, the librarian or passionate readers in the building are likely to be able to recommend some great titles! A final note about the Café: it is important to feature staff members as well as faculty; many times they may be hesitant to participate unless given some encouragement.

Poetry, Comic, and Magazine Breaks

Nothing creates a party atmosphere in school quite like a break in routine. A habit of mine became scheduling breaks in my instruction that would come off to the students as though they were totally impromptu diversions from formal teaching. One type of break was what I call a Poetry Break. No other genre seems to create quite the level of disdain that poetry does—especially in older readers. I fear that as students reach the point in school where they begin learning to analyze some poems, the joy of reading and performing them gets left behind; instead, we should have both.

In order for the Poetry Break to be effective, a large number of poetry books needs to be readily available in the classroom; it is best if they have a designated place in the room that is familiar to the students; this will save time when a Poetry Break is called. It is my strong recommendation that the poetry books of Shel Silverstein, Jack Prelutsky, Sara Holbrook, and Jeff Moss be among those in every collection. Of course, there are many others to include as well, but these are some of the poets whose work my students always find enjoyable.

A Poetry Break can last any amount of time, but mine tend to be between fifteen and twenty minutes. During that time, students can go anywhere in the room (or

out in the hall if the building lends itself to that) to get comfortable and enjoy poetry. They can read it silently or orally, they can read it aloud in pairs or triads, they
can practice a piece they want to perform for the class. And what am I doing while all
of this is going on? You already know, don't you? I'm doing exactly what they are doing—sometimes alone, sometimes with a partner, and sometimes with a group. One
of the most enjoyable parts of these breaks for me was being right in the middle of
a lesson and suddenly yelling "POETRY BREAK!" at the top of my lungs! Ha! The
students never had any idea when these were coming, and though my lesson plan
book told me, the students continued to think that these ideas just struck me from
out of the blue. Over the years, they learned to scramble from their desks quickly
and enjoy this spontaneous time of diversion with text. I found these breaks to place
poetry in a much more positive light. And then one day, I thought, "Why stop with
poetry? Why not expand the breaks to other genres that could suit my purposes?"

I was an only child (yes, mother, here I go again), and it was the pits a lot of the
time. When there's no one to play with or fight with, we only children sometimes
break down and read. Looking back, that is how I fell into the world of comic books.
I started with Archie and Richie Rich and graduated to X-Men and Batman. I was
never a serious collector, but I was a serious reader of comics, and my reading skills
grew quite strong as I devoured what some teachers call fluff every chance that I got.

What a wonderful moment when I held my first Comic Break in class! There was
no difference in the way this ran and the way a Poetry Break was conducted. I just
had to be certain there were lots of comic books around. Next, I tried Magazine
Breaks in the same format. It is amazing how many magazine companies will send
you a few old copies as samples! I wanted every kind of magazine imaginable—not
only to capture my students' interests, but to plant the seed that they could subscribe
to these magazines at home!

When I give seminars to parents on ways to help their kids become readers, one
of my biggest suggestions is that they allow each child in the house to subscribe to
a magazine of their choice. Moreover, it is important that the magazine arrive in the
child's name—not in either parent's name. Receiving mail gives a child ownership, and
when it's ownership in reading materials, that's a great situation. My magazine breaks at
school afforded me the opportunity to suggest that kids request a magazine subscrip-

tion from their parents. (Appendix B includes a few great magazine titles for kids.)

Over time, I combined different kinds of breaks on occasion, but not at first. It was important in the beginning for kids who had limited experience with magazines, for example, to spend some time with them so that they would learn what was out there. If I had allowed comic book or poetry reading during a Magazine Break, there would be little incentive for kids to explore the new genre of magazines. I need to take a moment here and caution readers not to generalize the comment I've just made to SSR or DEAR time. Those types of independent reading times are for kids to read self-selected text, in my opinion, of any type that is content appropriate. A "break" as described here is for the purpose of allowing kids to explore a specific genre for a short amount of time—so requiring that they interact with that specific genre is acceptable to me.

Newspaper Day

When I began publishing my writing several years ago, I was understandably thrilled. It was then that I decided I needed my students to experience this kind of rush as well. Thanks to *Writer Publications* (www.writerpublications.com), my wish came true in many cases—and I discovered yet another way to celebrate reading.

Writer Publications is responsible for the publication of three newspapers: *The Elementary School Writer, The Junior High School Writer,* and *The High School Writer.* Now, when I say "newspapers," I do mean newspapers. They look and feel like newspapers but are written entirely by kids from all over the country. Schools or individual classrooms can subscribe to one of the three specific editions and receive twenty-five copies each of the six times the newspaper is released throughout the school year; additional copies can be added to the subscription for larger class sizes. When I learned about these newspapers, I quickly got a sample copy and within a few weeks convinced my principal that I must have the money to take out a subscription (remember, one of my mottos is "Yes, there is too money!").

I lined up PTA mothers to bring treats six times a year, and we had Newspaper Day, when everyone sat around for a full forty-two minutes and had donuts, hot cocoa, juice—whatever—and read the newspaper! My students loved reading their peers' work when someone's story or poem had been accepted for publication. They enjoyed reading the writing of other kids from their age group around the country, and they also loved coming up with creative ideas for trying to get our class pictured in the paper—which we achieved! It was my final year of teaching in the public school when a student said to me, on Newspaper Day, "Hey! Dr. Layne, do you think next year we could have another kind of Newspaper Day as well as this one?" When I asked what he meant by that, he suggested that we have a day where we had lots of editions of different Chicagoland and local newspapers for kids to read from—what a great idea!

Club Read

Several years before book clubs were made popular (thank you, Ms. Winfrey), the American Library Association launched their own version of the idea with something called Club Read. They even had these nifty matching bags with a cool logo that said "Club Read." I saw the bag pictured in the ALA graphics catalog, my teacher's sense tingled, and I knew what I had to do.

When I taught fifth grade, there was a period of time during which we had adopted a new social studies program by Houghton Mifflin (I still remember), and we were excited. It was the first series that didn't seem to suggest we should cover history from the dawn of time all the way up to and including World War II for eleven- and twelve-year-olds in eight months. The program, basically, went from early American exploration through the Civil War. My colleagues and I immediately separated it out into four units: exploration and immigration, the American Revolution, the Westward Movement, and the Civil War. We also decided to each specialize in a unit and rotate the classes among the four of us; I had the American Revolution, which was an area of great interest to me.

As I began to prepare my content, I decided that it would be a good idea to supplement the reading my students would be doing in the textbook and the trade book we were using in class by giving them some choices of additional reading materials about the Revolutionary War. Thus, I explained to my principal, I needed money (some of you are catching on to a theme running through this book) to buy sets of books at various levels related to the Revolution and that I simply had to have these Club Read bags. I then created several books bags (each contained the same books) to go home with kids on a rotational basis throughout the unit. The bags were filled with picture books, nonfiction chapter books, historical fiction, short stories, and so forth, all related to our topic of study. Some of the titles were very simple reads while others would likely appeal only to my most gifted readers. I explained to my students that they were under no pressure to read anything from the bags that they didn't want to read; they didn't even have to take a bag home when their name was drawn. As soon as they heard they didn't have to read anything in the bag, what did everyone want to do? Take a bag home, of course! They could hardly wait for their names to be drawn! Isn't psychology great?

There was absolutely no kind of assessment with regard to this activity. I know some kids read the materials; they spoke too intelligently about things they found interesting and exciting or that challenged other information we had discussed from our textbook. I have a feeling some kids took the bag home and didn't read much or barely looked at the materials, but that was okay! Those who did nothing weren't any less informed than if I hadn't sent the Club Read bags home, but the ones who did read (and I believe that most did) gained more than if I had done nothing.

Picture Book of the Month

I have always been an avid reader of picture books. What's more, I am continually amazed at the number of teachers who don't use these little gems more frequently at all grade levels. No matter what your topic is or what you are trying to do, there's probably a picture book that will help you out!

When I worked in the early elementary grades, I learned quite quickly that any book in my hands was the book everyone wanted, so I decided to allow a little marketing common sense to help me out. I made a large sign that simply said, "Picture Book of the Month" and placed it on my desk along with a picture book sitting in a stand next to the sign. As was my habit, I made no announcement about it but waited for the questions. It took about ten minutes before the students had worked themselves into a bit of a frenzy about the book, at which point I offered an explanation.

Each month, a different picture book would be featured. Students could read the book during SSR, if they finished work early, during recess—any time that was appropriate. They could even check the book out overnight and have someone read to them, but only once each month. If they read it, they were invited to join me for lunch near the end of the month (everyone brought their own lunch—I brought brownies) and tell me what they thought of the story. On the last school day of each month, I would read the book aloud, explain why I selected it, and point out various features of the illustrations and the story line that I hoped they had noticed.

It was an instant hit! Students never seemed to tire of it over the years. Some years I used titles that supplemented another area of the curriculum, and one year I used all titles related to teaching and school. My students were especially wild about reading picture books focused on school because, of course, it is where they spend so much of their time.

When I moved to junior high school, the sign went with me! Though I changed the level of many of the picture books I was selecting, the enthusiasm from my students remained. Upon reflection, I wonder if having the Picture Book of the Month as part of my classroom routine helped these older students feel that it was okay to be looking at picture books. See Appendix C for some of my favorite Picture Book of the Month titles for use with younger and older kids, as well as a list of pictures books about school. Of course, junior high students were not going to join me at lunchtime as the elementary students had done, but a bonus point worked quite well as an incentive. Though innocuous with regard to final grades, what junior high school students won't do for one bonus point has yet to be truly verified.

FROM THE TRENCHES

Mrs. Hoochamadoochee was in rare form when she left a message on my voice mail at school that spring day. When receiving a call from a parent such as Mrs. H., you can always be sure of these three truths: (1) a tragedy beyond measure has struck young William; (2) you are either the person solely responsible for the calamity or the only one who can possibly save the day; and (3) a stirring call to action will be sounded directing you to respond within a nanosecond to prevent a reduction in William's self-esteem.

As I listened to her three lengthy voice-mail messages (she kept calling back, but does that surprise you?), I was somewhat relieved to hear that in this particular situation I would not be playing the role of the villain but rather the role of the misguided teacher. It seemed I had not given her sound advice four months earlier, and it was time to tell me all about it. I gathered a wide assortment of aids about me (hot chocolate, bottled water, root beer, vegetables and dip, Lifesavers, a bagel, chips and salsa, a peanut butter and banana sandwich, a bottle of aspirin, and some antacid pills) and prepared to return the call.

In late November, we had spoken in person because William was not reading nearly enough at home to suit Mrs. H. I had made several suggestions, and she immediately latched onto the idea of a magazine subscription for her boy. I recommended that the magazine be centered on a topic of interest to William and that it be specifically addressed to him when it came in the mail. Despite my cautioning her that this was only one strategy and that it might take some time, she left the meeting and was bounding down the hallway of the school in no time, declaring me a literacy genius to anyone who would stop and listen.

Now, based on her three hysteria-laden voice mails, it appeared I had fallen from grace. Mrs. H. was relieved, of course, that I returned her call so quickly.

"What seems to be the trouble, Mrs. H.?" I asked calmly.

"WILLIAM! William is the trouble, Dr. Layne!" She was screeching. "I have tried your magazine idea for a few months, and it *never* has worked one time! This is terrible, Dr. Layne, TERRIBLE! What can we do?"

I thought to mention that children in other parts of the world were missing limbs due to roadside bombs but then thought better of it. I had promised my principal I would work on what he called my "penchant for saying the wrong thing" to hysterical parents. My spider sense told me this could be one of those times, and I decided to make him proud. "What happened the first time the magazine arrived?" I queried. I felt certain I sounded exceedingly courteous.

Her explanation of what happened on the day the first magazine arrived had me reaching for the antacid pills. Long story short—she should have been arrested for stalking her own child. (But I didn't say that to her. The principal, I reminded myself, the principal.) It sounded as though she had thrust the magazine into his hands the minute he arrived home from school, trumpeted the virtues of reading this magazine, pointed out how she had addressed it to him, insisted that he begin reading it immediately, followed him around the house until he sat down with it, and then watched him while he tried to read. After repeating this process for four months she was confounded as to why he did not appear at all pleased when his monthly magazine arrived.

"Well, now, Mrs. H.," I was sure my voice radiated charm, "I think we are going to have to become *strategic* with William. What we are going to do," I explained stealthily, "is use the skill of *subtlety*." I heard a sharp intake of air on the other end of the receiver.

"Really?" Her breath was a whisper.

"Yes," I quietly responded. "The next time the magazine arrives, I would like you to leave it on his bed or his desk and then do . . . *nothing*."

"Nothing!" She became loud. She was flabbergasted. "But if I don't tell him . . ."

"Mrs. H., remember what I said—you're going to be *strategic*! Your strategy is highly complex for the very reason that it involves you failing to interact with your child. Trust me," I begged. "He won't be able to believe it is happening."

The call actually turned out to be one of our shorter ones—I had half of the food supply still left. She came on board with my idea then soared with excitement, as was typical, thanked me repeatedly, and promised to let me know how things were going sometime soon.

A month later she showed up after school with no appointment. (Do people do that to other professionals?) Her jubilation could not be contained. The strategy of leaving William alone, she was convinced, had led him to read the magazine! "He read it cover to cover, Dr. Layne! Really! The whole thing—in one sitting! It took him nearly an hour, and he never looked up once. When he found it on his bed, he flipped it open and read straight through."

"Why, Mrs. H., that certainly is exciting! What good news. Sometimes kids just need to have the adults in their lives avoid a tendency some of us might have to *hover*. Don't you think?"

"Oh, Dr. Layne, I couldn't agree more." She nodded emphatically. "They were talking about those parents on Oprah the other day! They call them helicopter parents. Did you know that?"

I had to let that one go, or I was sure to lose my job. I decided to reinforce my point with excitement. "When we loosen up the reigns a bit, sometimes the kids just start to fly, Mrs. H.! I am curious about one thing, though (and I really was). How did you know William read the whole magazine in one sitting if he was in his bedroom the entire time? Did he say something when he came out?"

"Oh, no!" she remarked. "He didn't say anything, but I was watching him through the keyhole in his bedroom door the whole time."

Angels and ministers of grace, defend us.

Mr. Schubert, my sixth-grade teacher, helped make me a reader by doing nothing. One afternoon we sat in the bright classroom engaged in our daily quiet reading time. Around me kids read *Island of the Blue Dolphins* and *Call It Courage*. I read *Superman.* As one might imagine, comics were not in the approved reading curriculum, but as Mr. Schubert came to my desk, he looked down, saw what I was reading . . . and walked by. The memory is fuzzy, but I think he may have even nodded.

I tell stories with pictures and words and it's always been that way. I was probably as bright as the kid reading in the next desk over, but the abstract world of little marks on paper never seemed real enough to me. I read the world first in images—in a progression of pictures that added up to some understanding. From Superman, I quickly moved on to Edgar Rice Burroughs, E. Nesbit, and Madeleine L'Engle. Images led me into these written stories and eventually to the riches of storytelling of every kind. I continued to struggle with the written word—I'm still a slow reader—but Mr. Schubert recognized that simply walking by would open a door, and that any open door is a way in.

—*Eric Rohmann*

CHAPTER 9

Oh, Author, Where Art Thou? Igniting a Passion Through Author Visits

Students should hear from and speak to an author several times throughout their school career. There, I said it. I haven't read it in anyone else's books yet, and I needed to be sure it was said. I realize that the fact that I am an author of children's and young adult books is going to lead some readers to say, "Well, of course Layne would say that! He's drumming up business for himself and his friends." To any who have rushed to that conclusion, I'd like to point out that I was hosting author visits as a classroom teacher long before I was ever an author myself. They were a lot of work—but worth the effort because of all the excitement they generated around reading and writing. As a classroom teacher, I considered the promoting of reading and writing to be my job; thus, advocating for author visits was, in my opinion, a nonnegotiable part of my self-made job description. And they were much more effective than assigning every student in my class to write to an author. Can I tell you that many authors hate that? Think about it. How would you like to get a letter written by someone who was only writing to you because some authority figure made him do it? Now, how about thirty, sixty, or ninety letters from people who were assigned to write to you, and they all say, "Please write back," despite the fact that the letters contain nothing of substance to which you could even respond because the kids didn't write from the heart? No, an author visit, bringing the voice behind the print to life, is the way you connect kids with authors— not through a letter-writing assignment that is likely to disappoint everyone involved.

Trying to gain support for an author visit to a junior or senior high school appears to be, in most cases, a much larger battle than at the elementary level. From both my own experience visiting schools as an author and from the feedback provided by many colleagues and booksellers, it is clear that the largest number of author visits takes place in elementary schools. It is, of course, a grand thing for these little tykes to be meeting authors and to begin seeing themselves as authors. But I am baffled that the closer in age our students get to actually becoming more competent writers, the closer they get to reaching an age where they are thinking about career options, the less teachers and schools seem inclined to promote and fund author visits. In my dream world (this would be the dream school mentioned in Chapter 5 magnified now to the point that I am taking over education across the globe, and everyone is doing it my way), every senior high school student would have the opportunity to hear from an author once a year. Junior high school students would hear from authors twice during their time in junior high, and elementary students would hear from an author every other year.

Should we not be concerned that the next great authors could be sitting in our schools right now? Would it be so horrible if one day—when they are speechwriters for the president of the United States, screenwriters with Steven Spielberg, or best-selling novelists—that they recognize your school's or district's author visitation program as a linchpin in their career decision? In my dream world, those of you who work so hard to plan and organize the author visits are also invited to the Oprah Winfrey Show where you are thanked in person by your former (now famous) student and Oprah, who then presents you with a brand-new automobile.

Author visits are exciting! A visit from an author can expose students to the wonders of reading and writing in a unique way, one they may have never considered before. When authors come to speak to young people, they often inspire them to want to read great books and to write with more consideration for their audience. There's no denying that preparing for author visits is a lot of work, but in my experience, the benefits have always been worth the effort.

Before I hosted my first author visit, I did a lot of reading and research on how to make it a truly significant event in the lives of my students. I wanted to light a fire for reading and writing in them through this author visit, and I knew that meant careful and calculated planning on my part. Over the years, I continued to refine what I learned from sponsoring those first author visits and added to my knowledge base when I later began visiting schools as an author myself.

My first rule of thumb is to know the author! Of course, I don't mean that you have to know him or her personally, but don't ask everybody and their brother to shell out $2,000 so you can bring an author to the school simply because you like his or her book. What are you going to do if the PTA supplies half of the money you need and their board members show up to hear your author, who clearly has no rapport whatsoever with kids and no level of skill in the realm of public speaking? You want to have heard the author speak, if at all possible. You also want to ask for and check references. In my experience, most authors who speak well to teachers also speak well with kids; however, I no longer automatically assume that to be true.

Several years ago, I heard a fellow children's author speak at a teachers' convention. He was magnificent—the crowd was wild for him. Later, he was visiting in my area and asked if I could help recommend some schools where he might visit. I heartily agreed to do so. My jaw dropped a few months later when a principal friend called to tell me that the author I had recommended had been terribly unkind to a child with disabilities in front of the entire school, and that he clearly had no idea how to interact with kids. I swore that was a lesson I would never have to learn again; if I haven't heard or seen an author work with kids, I need to talk to someone who has or I won't bring him or her in.

Many authors have "guestbooks" on their Web sites that can provide solid references; remember, you don't have to leave a comment to visit a guestbook. You can, instead, see what comments others are leaving. Most authors will welcome your request for references because it shows you are interested in quality. If you need a number to make a phone call or need an e-mail address, look for a "contact" button on the author's Web site and make your request known. It is always a good idea to do a thorough review of an author's Web site before contacting him or her. One reason is that you may find answers to many of your questions on the site; another reason is that you will impress the author or his or her agent if it is clear from interacting with you that you have done your homework. The easiest way to make contact with an author is generally through his or her Web site. Don't know it? Google the author's name, and a link will likely appear. Most authors who are willing to visit schools do have a Web site. If you cannot find a site, you can always contact the author's publisher to see whether he or she visits schools. A general rule of thumb: the harder it is to contact someone, the less likely that individual is to agree to public appearances.

Honorariums and Funding

Honorariums vary from author to author and are subject to increases just like the costs involved in any service. Don't assume an author's honorarium based on what someone else says or based on a quote you were given at some other point in time. If an author's honorarium is beyond your budget, politely explain that this is the case and be prepared to close the conversation. If the author or his or her representative is willing to negotiate the honorarium, let them offer. Most of us don't go to the store and ask for a service to be less than the advertised cost. Treat the author's honorarium similarly.

There are a variety of ways to fund an author visit. One way is through the local PTA. Work with the PTA to brainstorm creative ways to fund your author event. Host a craft fair, bake sale, or car wash. You are only as limited as your imagination. How about selling donuts before school in the morning? Another method of funding an author visit is through grants from state reading associations, local reading councils, or literary organizations. Silent or live auctions held during curriculum night or at some other large parent gathering have frequently garnered funds for such events and become something the school community looks forward to each year. Some items that can be auctioned don't require a lot of expense and preparation: special parking places at school (with signs); your child can be "Principal for a Day" or "Secretary for a Day"; teachers can auction a volleyball or kickball game after school, to be played against the winning bidder and his or her team. The possibilities abound.

In addition to state literacy organizations, another great place to go for grant information is state arts councils! The premiere Web site that will help you gain information on the state arts councils is www.nasaa-arts.org. On the home page there was, at the time of this publication, a "member directory" icon in the far upper-left-hand corner with a small U.S. map. When you click on the icon, a large map appears. By selecting your state, you will come up with contact information for the arts council in your state! This is a gold mine, linking you to a place that may indeed have some grant funding available for your author visit! You can also contact the national office via U.S. mail, phone, fax, and e-mail:

National Assembly of State Arts Agencies
1029 Vermont Avenue, NW, 2nd Floor
Washington, DC 20005
202/347-6352 Ph
202/737-0526 Fax
nasaa@nasaa-arts.org

Paying the Author

Many authors support their families in large part through income derived from visiting schools. Be prepared to pay the author on time. Schools often require a payment notice a month or more in advance in order to prepare a check. Be on top of this, and be sure any expenses that are to be covered are provided for in the check. The author may be counting on being paid for his or her service on the day of the visit, and this needs to be honored. Think how you would feel if you were told, "Your paycheck is unavailable because someone forgot to issue it; can you wait another few weeks?" I have never failed to pay a visiting author on time when I was the host, yet despite signed contracts, I have, as a visiting author myself, been paid late for a myriad of reasons. It is a simple and sad truth that many people are unconcerned with paying someone for a service once the service has been completed. Don't let this happen when you are in charge—and don't make your guest ask to be paid. There will be a lot of excitement on the day of the author visit, and the person or people sponsoring the visit are likely to be giddy with details. Think, What can be done to be sure that payment is not forgotten? Also, never place a check in a goodie basket and then fail to tell the author it is in there. I have heard of such baskets being delivered to the wrong hotel room, being thrown away before they were completely emptied, and so on. Avoid what could become a disaster story with you playing one of the major roles.

Travel/Hotel Arrangements

Most authors prefer to make their own travel arrangements with regard to flights because they know more about their availability for flights, airlines, and so forth. Still, you will need to know this information eventually if a flight is involved in the visit. A visiting author is a guest. Some authors prefer rental cars to allow more control over where and when they go, but it is quite courteous to offer to pick up your author at the airport if he or she is flying in. This is much more personal and friendly than asking him or her to rent a car, wait for a commercial shuttle, or take a cab in what might be a strange city.

When picking the author up, do not assume that he or she wants a tour of the city, to go sightseeing, or to have dinner with your family. Be sensitive to the fact that authors are frequently surrounded by people when they are traveling and may want some down time when they arrive. Your visiting author may be working on a book and be looking forward to time in the hotel alone to write. You can always offer opportunities without making your guest feel obligated.

When booking the hotel room, ask if the author prefers a smoking or nonsmoking room or has any additional hotel room requests. Providing a list of nearby hotels from which your guest author might choose is sure to be appreciated. It is always good to remember that you may be dealing with someone who is away from his or her own bed a great deal. While you might think the beds at Motel 6 are dandy when vacationing, the need for a quality bed and good rest is different when you are addressing large audiences the next morning. Be sure the hotel room is paid for in advance by the school district. Selecting a hotel with a restaurant inside may be greatly appreciated by your author. Making an appointment to speak personally with the manager of one of the nicer hotels in your area could easily get you a significant discount on a wonderful room for your guest. Ask if the hotel would partner with the school in this effort to inspire local children! Tell the manager you will mention the hotel's support in the newsletter or the local paper, and then send him or her a copy.

Presentation Needs

All authors vary in their presenting style. Your author may use or need a slide projector, a microphone, a laptop and LCD projector, an overhead projector, a CD player, a DVD player, or a combination of these. The author might require an Internet connection or sound from a laptop. How wonderful if you are "in the know" well in advance so that everything is ready on presentation day. Having power strips and extension cords at the ready is a tremendous help. Also, researching the lighting in the presentation area in advance and knowing how and where to turn on/off various sets of lights can save valuable time. Any equipment the school has agreed to provide should be tested and ready in advance of the author's arrival.

Find out how many sessions an author is willing to provide in a day as well as the session length, number of students in the audience, and grade levels the author is willing to manage. All this information should be agreed to in writing and a schedule should be prepared for the author in advance. It is *not* appropriate to change the agreement with the author. He or she is arriving prepared to do what was agreed to, and no significant changes should be made on short notice without the author's explicit consent.

Preparing Students

Visiting authors agree that the most important way to ensure a successful author visit is to make sure the students have read the author's books. Be prepared by having the school librarian order multiple copies of the books. Post a list of the author's titles in the library. Ask many teachers in the building to read some of the author's books aloud and give book talks based on the author's titles in advance of the visit. Encourage classes to visit the author's Web site to learn about the author and maybe bring back an interesting fact to share with the class.

Post signs and flyers around the school to spread the word that the author is coming. Ask students to prepare a list of questions to ask the author. Review the questions with your students the day before the visit. When you ask an author what has made their most successful school visits stand out, their responses are always linked to how well the kids know their books and how strong the questions were.

Ordering and Autographing Books

Author visits that include book-signing events create much enthusiasm and excitement. This is the student's golden opportunity to exchange a few words with an author one-on-one and to receive a signed book. Scheduling time for autographing is important to many students, and it is a way to witness firsthand the level of excitement generated by all your hard work. Most authors prefer to sign only their books—as opposed to slips of paper, shoes, shoulders, backpacks, or T-shirts. Ask your guest in advance about this—and notify the students so that the author is not placed in an uncomfortable situation.

It is important to order books well in advance of the author's visit. Many local booksellers as well as book publishing companies offer a significant discount on books purchased in advance of an author visit, but it takes *time* to process the order. Also, most booksellers and/or publishers will not charge you for the books when they are ordered, allowing you thirty days or more before you need to pay for them; often, you will also be allowed to return those books you have not sold. Discuss this in detail with the bookseller or publisher and find out who covers the costs for shipping books back and forth.

It is a fact that several students will fail to preorder books. Then, they will get very excited the day of the visit and come asking to order books "now." You should anticipate this and congratulate yourself. What this really means is that a student who thought having an author come would not be a big deal now thinks that it is a big deal and wants to read! When preordering books, ask the bookseller or publisher if the discount you are receiving applies if you place another order following the author's visit. In many cases, the answer will be yes. If you have labels ready, the author may be able to sign and personalize labels for those kids who failed to preorder, and you can hold that signed label until the student brings you the money for the book(s) he or she wants you to order.

Some publishing houses—or sometimes the authors themselves—have a letter to help organize books sales to parents. This letter should be sent home with the students so that the parents can have time to select titles for purchase. It also helps the school order what is needed so that money can be saved on shipping costs. Have students pay for the books in advance so that no money will have to be exchanged at the event. Keep in mind that while paperbacks keep costs down, hardbacks make treasured keepsakes.

Ask the author which title(s) he or she would like you to have available at the event. Also, ask if certain titles will be focused on during the visit, and plan your book order accordingly.

Publicizing and Generating Excitement

You may want to organize a publicity committee of faculty, staff, PTA members, and students to help build the excitement. Ask each member to find creative ways to promote the event. Posters, publicity photos, flyers, review copies of new titles, and other promotional materials will often be furnished by the publisher once an event is scheduled. He or she who does not *ask* does not *receive!* Ask the librarian to showcase the author's books in the library or in a display. Have the committee send a press release to your local paper announcing the event and invite them to come. Remember, always ask permission from the author before scheduling a media event the day of the visit.

Setting Up a Hospitality Crew

You may want to make a guest author feel welcome by having a crew of teachers, parents, faculty, and students on hand to give a hearty reception. Create displays, ask the community to get involved, and hold a small luncheon with the author's favorite foods! Be sure when planning any type of meal event that you check for dietary restrictions. You can ask your local grocery store or restaurant to donate food in exchange for publicity at the event. Allow those teachers who have worked to promote the author's visit to attend a special lunch with the author. Remember, lunch is to be a break for the author—large groups of people at lunchtime may not be restful.

The most hospitable thing that you can do is to have one person, someone who knows the school well, serving as host/hostess for the day. When the person in the know has classes to teach, bus duty to supervise, or meetings to attend, it sends a message that you may not intend. Don't pass your guest off to someone else every forty minutes of the day or, worse yet, leave your guest to fend for him/herself. While some of you are aghast to think of anyone doing such a thing, it happens more often than you would guess because the school refused to grant a substitute to free up the person who has planned the entire event. Ask for this from the very beginning!

HOT TIPS FOR A GREAT SCHOOL VISIT: A QUICK REVIEW OF KEY ITEMS

- Before you invite the press, check with the author.
- Stick to the schedule that was discussed. Switching the audience planned or changing the timing can wreak havoc on a planned presentation.
- Before you set up a video, please ask permission to do so. Some people are camera shy and are very uncomfortable being videotaped.
- Don't assume the author wants to have dinner with your great-aunt Marge or a tour of the local pottery factory. Offer opportunities in a way that does not make him or her feel obligated.
- Make sure you stick to your time schedule. Allow enough time between sessions and at the end of the day to get the author to the airport if necessary.
- If your guest is driving in, where is he or she going to park? Will he or she be trapped by buses when it is time to leave?
- Check dietary restrictions.
- Have the honorarium ready and in the correct amount plus expenses.
- Have the presentation area and supplies set up in advance.
- Order books and schedule time for autographing.
- Familiarize students with the author and his or her books.

A Handy Timetable to Help You Get Organized

THE DAY BEFORE

Make sure the space where the event will be held is clean and contains enough electrical outlets and extension cords.

Check your equipment for burned-out bulbs, slide carousels that stick, or microphones that are not working. Do you have a microphone stand? Does the clip on the stand actually hold the type of microphone you intend to put into it?

Make sure you have plenty of seating and that the teachers know when they are scheduled for their author visit. Kids in the upper grades who are seated in chairs make a *much* more attentive audience.

Check with all of your committee members to make sure they know their assignments.

THE DAY OF

The day is here and everything should be running smoothly. It's up to you and another point person to keep the event running on schedule.

Make sure you have the author's payment ready and give it to him or her promptly. *Don't* make your author ask to be paid.

During both the author's presentation and autographing, make sure you have a bottle of water handy. If the name of the person to whom the book is to be signed can be printed neatly on a sticky note or autograph slip, long lines may be defeated!

To keep the lines moving along, have a person assigned to open the book to the correct page for the author to sign.

THE DAY AFTER

Have a discussion about the event. Ask for feedback. How could it have been better? What did you learn? Start planning your next author visit!

FROM THE TRENCHES

I have visited a lot of schools as a guest author over the past several years. I have fond memories of many of those visits, such as the one at my dear friend Renee Boisseau's small school in Kila, Montana, set against the beautiful backdrop of the mountains; The Rowan-Salisbury elementary schools of North Carolina where they brought *live* sheep to school to celebrate two of my books; laughing the day and night away with my pals at Sky View Middle School in Colorado Springs, Colorado; the annual visit with seventh graders at my adopted school, Dundee Middle School in West Dundee, Illinois; and, of course, the visits to each school of "The Sisters" in Washington State. (Gail's school had the largest autographing at an elementary building in my career—Go Meridian Elementary!) But of all the visits that I have made to schools, the most memorable to date have been to the schools on the island of Guam.

In 2004, I visited the island for nearly two weeks and worked with children in the local elementary, middle, and high schools. I found the teachers on the island to be every bit as dedicated and passionate as the teachers on the mainland here in the United States; however, in most cases, they had far less to work with when it came to resources. I recall my friend Rowena Dimla as she described how a storm had nearly wiped out her entire classroom; only a few of her books had survived the storm. "It is what we do," she said, "we keep going." The spirit of these teachers was amazing to me. While schools in parts of the mainland might well be ravaged at times by the weather, I had never considered that island schools must deal with this quite regularly. Many of my friends on Guam had been dealt multiple blows by storms over the years, and yet their spirit and dedication to the children was indomitable.

One evening, I was invited to Guam's St. Francis School. I had been told that the school's choir was quite famous and that they were to sing prior to my presentation. Little did I know what was about to happen. To this day, I have never been more moved by a performance. There were tears streaming down my face. When they asked me to come up and begin,

I could not do so. I literally could not rise from my chair. I requested that the choir sing an encore. I still remember my words to the crowd following the musical encore I had requested of the children. I looked at the audience and said, "I have never been less interested in anything I have to say than I am at this moment." It remains true today. This is a moment "from the trenches" that is seared into my memory.

In reflecting on it all again for the writing of this book, I believe my uncharacteristic "failure to launch" occurred because I was in a situation where I was supposed to be giving and yet, surprisingly, I was the recipient of something much greater than I had the power to repay. And isn't that the way it is—so often—for those of us who work with kids? We spend our entire career giving to them—late into the night, up at the crack of dawn, during our twenty-minute lunch break—whatever it takes. We give and give and give to make a difference, and somewhere along the road we come to that almost-tangible realization that our students have, somehow, magically contributed more to our lives than we would ever have been able to give them—no matter how many years we taught.

RECEIVING A WARM WELCOME IN GUAM

She was my mother's eighth-grade English teacher and mine as well. I was in her class the year before she retired. She had a crazy white crop of hair, and her voice could shake the rafters. I sat in the front row that remarkable, terrifying, complicated year. Miss Huff would dress like a pirate and read the part of Long John Silver with her craggy bellow that shivered your timbers. When we began *The Good Earth,* wildly famous in my junior high because of the sexual reference, she stood in front of us and said, "For those of you who don't know, go to page _____ and it's there. Now let's get on with the power of the book."

From *The Good Earth*, I learned about locusts and how they destroy and swoop in like an army in the clouds and take everything a person has worked for. As I got older, I had a few times in life when it seemed like surely the locusts had filled the sky and settled on my life and ate away at it until there didn't seem to be much left. And I remembered Miss Huff reading that scene, her voice thick with the pain of loss—this missionary of reading. We simply had to get it; we had to feel it and understand. "You see it, don't you?" she'd shout. It was no use lying because she would ask then, how—how did we see it and what did it mean? It meant, in part, that books and characters were alive, that fiction was so very, very real. So real, people would jump from the pages and run around the room and never leave our hearts.

Joan Bauer

Photo by Jim Lundquist

She was the one who handed me *To Kill a Mockingbird*. "You're ready for this," she said. "Come talk to me when you've finished it." It remains my favorite book of all time. She gave me Joseph Conrad and she told me over and over not to read *Gatsby* too early. So I waited until sophomore year and gobbled it up. And I believe that somehow she's sat with me and every book I've read since. I can hear her prodding me, saying, "But why, Joan? Why did you love it? What does that mean?" I loved Miss Huff and sometimes she scared me to death. She had the fire. It lit up her eyes and roared out of her mouth. She shook thoughts from me, she burned books into me, and branded me forever.

— *Joan Bauer*

CHAPTER 10

Making the Intangible Tangible: Igniting a Passion with a Quarterly Plan

Let's be honest. Most people want a plan to follow—a road map of sorts. I have tried to make the case throughout this book that the affective elements of reading instruction are generally disregarded in most curricular initiatives. The strategies mentioned here are not likely to show up in a packaged program, a basal series, or even in some set of state, provincial, or national standards. It's not always that people don't want to address the issue; it's more often that they don't know they need to—or they don't know how.

My chief goal in my professional writing is to promote thought that leads to change that will ultimately impact instruction. The strategies outlined throughout the first nine chapters of this book are designed to help teachers, administrators, and other educational leaders on their way. I am aware, though, that there may be some who will ask a reasonable question: How do I fit all these strategies in? Tackling that question is daunting, and any answer to it would be ridiculous; thus, I refuse to answer. Instead, I will tackle a similar but safer question: How *might* I fit *several* of these strategies in?

There are likely teachers at multiple grade levels—primary through high school—reading this book. Thinking about the different structures of your schedules, varying time allotments for literacy instruction, range of populations served, and on and on, it would be ludicrous to try to suggest one way to make it all happen. What I have tried to do is lay out a quarterly schedule that could be used as a foundation for those of you who are interested in teaching the love of reading. I gave you a Monday through Friday schedule for just nine weeks. Of course, there will be holidays, early-release days, I'm-losing-it-and-I-think-I-just-need-to-be-a-greeter-at-Wal-Mart-days, so the schedule is not even close to perfect. If you know me, you would know that this was hard for me to do because my dream is *not* that you will try to force this schedule into your framework. No, my dream is that your team, your building, your district will use what I am providing to begin conversations about how it could reasonably look and efficiently work in your classrooms, your building, your district. Thus, as you move forward and look at the schedule, remind yourself of what you just read. This is not do or die. Steven Layne is not saying, "If you don't do it just this way, all students will leave school and hate reading forevermore." Middle school and high school language arts/literature/English teachers, please understand that I scheduled this as if you all had eighty to ninety minutes every single day for language arts instruction. I know some of you have only forty-two minutes, but I decided to lay this out the way it *should* be done. Please do me a favor and ask the administration or parents if they mind if math and science are combined into one forty-two-minute period. If you are expected to teach both reading and writing in forty-two minutes, why can't other subjects be combined in a similar manner? In case no one noticed, reading and writing are two different subjects. I just really want to lead a revolt over this issue, but that's for another time.

I also want to remind my readers that in the schedule that follows there is no mention of the other half of that reading circle I introduced in Chapter 1. In other words, there is no mention in this schedule of direct instruction of reading skills. Why? Because I am hoping you already have a plan in place for that. The idea in creating true readers is that we teach the "skill" and we teach the "will." I am hoping you will decide how to integrate the "will" part into your reading instruction in whatever way works best for you, remembering that the skill and the will are, in my humble opinion, *equally necessary* if we want to create true readers.

I have listed the chapter where each of the strategies outlined in the schedule is discussed in detail so that you can easily flip back for further reading when you find yourself saying, "What is he talking about?" Bullet points are quick reminders that may keep you from having to flip back and reread as often. I outlined this quarterly schedule for the first nine weeks of school; thus, you would not necessarily be repeating some of these strategies (like an interest inventory) in the second nine weeks, nor in the third or the fourth.

WEEK 1

MONDAY

Dr. Layne's Hot Read Sign, Book Stand, and Book in Stand (Chapter 5)

- Use your name, not mine, because they like you better.
- The book in the book stand is the one you are currently reading—written for your grade level of students. It is not the book you are reading aloud to them (that's another book). This is the book you are reading to further your knowledge of books at this level. When you finish, you will move on to another one.

Discussion of What Is Involved in Previewing a Book (Chapter 5)

- You will be introducing and reviewing one preview skill each day. Today, since you are beginning, you may introduce two or three different preview skills.
- Let students know to expect a five-minute mini-lesson on preview skills daily.
- Once you have taught all the previewing skills you can think of—which will likely use up two or three weeks, you repeat one each day. Over time this only takes a few minutes because students come to learn them so well.

Interest Inventories Taken by Students and Collected (Chapter 2)

- You will likely only administer these at the beginning of the year. Possibly midyear for an update if you decide this is of interest to you.

Meet with Librarian to Select Target Student 1 (Chapter 2)

- You will use interest inventory information in attempt to reach Target Student 1.

Students Take Initial Reading Survey (Chapter 2)

Introduce and Begin Read–Aloud Book 1 (Chapter 4)

- You may also be reading aloud picture books from time to time; however, when I discuss read-aloud books in this schedule, I am always referring to a chapter book or a novel, and all grade levels could have one of these ongoing.
- You want a book that will *grab them*. Remember you build trust and confidence with the first two to three chapter books/novels you read aloud.
- You want to launch your book well. You may devote more time to the opening one to three days of a new read-aloud than you will normally give over to this activity. If you don't grab them all at the launch, you will leave some behind for the rest of the story.

TUESDAY

Book Preview Mini-Lesson (Chapter 5)

Introduce Someday Book List/Books to Consider List (Chapter 5)

- Sections may include *From Book Chats, From Shopping, From Read Arounds, From Recommendations*

Teacher/Librarian Book Chats (Chapter 3)

- Give at least two book chats. Five or six is great but not always possible if you are new at this. From now on, whenever it says "book chats," the recommendation is to provide at least two.
- The fewer books you are chatting, the more copies of each title it would be ideal to have available. How sad if you get twenty-three students excited about only three titles and there is only one copy of each in the whole school.
- If you are chatting in the library, have the titles out and available for checkout. If you are not in the library, work out a time for kids to be able to get their hands on them for checkout.
- Remind kids that they can also look for these titles at bookstores and the public library.
- Will the librarian give book talks with you? You can introduce more titles this way!
- Student should have their Someday Book Lists or Books to Consider sheets out whenever they are listening to book chats.

Continue Read-Aloud

- The amount of time spent on the read-aloud each day must vary due to your specific teaching situation. Are you in the launch right now? If so, it needs more time than normal!

WEDNESDAY

Introduce *First Read Club* (Chapter 8)

- If this is a classroom First Read Club, you really need no advance publicity. You can announce today and start tomorrow if you have some new books ready. If this will be a First Read Club run through the library, you need posters up in advance of the first meeting, announcements made in classes, and so on.

Continue Read-Aloud

Book Preview Mini-Lesson

THURSDAY

Read Around (Chapter 8)
- Review previewing skills introduced thus far
- Hardcover books only

Continue Read-Aloud

Book Preview Mini-Lesson

First Read Club Meets and Selects Books to Read (not during class time) (Chapter 8)

FRIDAY

Meet with Librarian and Target Student 1 (not during class time) (Chapter 2)
- Books and other reading materials based on Target Student 1's interest must already be pulled and ready.
- Remember to say or show: I (or we) thought of you.

Book Preview Mini-Lesson

WEEK 2

Note on Read-Alouds: By the time the *launch* of Read-Aloud 1 is successfully completed, it will often be necessary for middle school or high school teachers to read aloud three days per week as opposed to daily. I will be listing read-aloud time as three times per week throughout the remaining weeks with the caveat that the elementary teachers understand that for them it should be *every day*—even though it is not specified that way here. The schedule will also read as though a whole quarter is devoted to completing one read-aloud. For those who complete several read-alouds in a quarter: each time you complete one, you may wish to use some of the concluding reminders contained at the end of Week 9 in this schedule.

MONDAY

Introduce the Golden Recommendation Shelf (Chapter 8)
- Have enough stock ready so that it does not become emptied as soon as it begins!

Take the Status of the Class (Chapter 6)
- Remember to give *your* status report to open this. You want to accentuate speed on this when first introducing it. The goal is that eventually this is so routine students can really move through it quickly.

- You will be stopping now and then for a public-private conversation.

Continue Read-Aloud

Book Preview Mini-Lesson

TUESDAY

Teacher/Librarian Book Chats

Buzz About Books (Chapter 6)
- Assign groups for this rather than allowing kids to form groups.
- You are always part of a group or two for this. Don't try to get to every group because you are more disruptive than anything. It's okay for you not to be everywhere.

Drop Everything and Read (D.E.A.R.) (or Zip Your Lips and Read [Z.Y.L.A.R.]or Sustained Silent Reading [S.S.R.] or Whatever You Call It)
- You decide length of time. In many cases, you will be targeting growth over time in how long they can sustain this reading time.
- This time is critical as you initiate more and more strategies. If you want them to be successful, kids need time to read in school as well as outside of it. For example, Status of the Class is tough to keep successfully going if all the reading they are doing is expected to be done at home.
- If you aren't going to read, too (YES, the WHOLE time), then don't bother with D.E.A.R. time for the students.
- Any type of reading is fine as long as text is appropriate.

Book Preview Mini-Lesson

WEDNESDAY

Continue Read-Aloud

Freewrite About Books (Chapter 6)
- Will you collect these to read through, will a few students share at the podium, will kids read these aloud to people in their buzz groups? Always have an audience in mind for this. No grade other than participation.

D.E.A.R.

Book Preview Mini-Lesson

THURSDAY

Introduce Goal Setting for Reading (Chapter 2)

- Brainstorm types of goals
- Realistic but stretching goals
- Time to begin thinking/developing in class
- Due tomorrow

Continue Read-Aloud

Status of the Class

D.E.A.R.

Book Preview Mini-Lesson

FRIDAY

Introduce Reading Logs (Chapter 5)

- You are going to have one of these as well—hang it in a public place.
- If you can make a giant one for your door or hallway bulletin board, the entire school can be kept abreast of what you are reading and what you think about these titles!
- Please list the children's/young adult titles you are reading here. Do not list adult reads with inappropriate content for the students you are teaching. That is not the purpose.

Record Reading Goals

Buzz About Books

D.E.A.R.

- I often make this a bit longer on Friday than on other days. Keep this in mind.

Book Preview Mini-Lesson

WEEK 3

MONDAY

Introduce Picture Book of the Month (Chapter 8)

- This should always begin and end close to the beginning and end of a month. I scheduled this as if you were in school for the first two weeks of August, which makes Week 3 the first week of September. Adjust as necessary.

Status of the Class

Continue Read-Aloud

Book Preview Mini-Lesson

TUESDAY

Teacher/Librarian Book Chats

Buzz About Books

D.E.A.R.

Book Preview Mini-Lesson

WEDNESDAY

Continue Read-Aloud

Freewrite About Books

Check with a Few Students on Reading Goals

D.E.A.R.

Book Preview Mini-Lesson

THURSDAY

Continue Read-Aloud

Status of the Class

Check with a Few Students on Reading Goals

D.E.A.R.

Book Preview Mini-Lesson

FRIDAY

Update Reading Logs

Shopping Trip 1 in the Library (Chapter 5)

- Schedule with librarian well in advance.
- Set time limit on "quiet" shopping time before entering, followed by a nice amount of time for talking, sharing, and book checkout.
- Remind students they are about to use their previewing skills while they shop.

D.E.A.R.
- Can you imagine just completing a shopping trip and then being given no time to enjoy what you "bought"?

Book Preview Mini-Lesson

WEEK 4

MONDAY

Magazine Break (Chapter 8)
- Have kids' magazines at many levels—old issues are fine, too. Garage sales are a gold mine. Does the library have some subscriptions? Can they initiate ongoing subscriptions and give you the old ones each year?

Status of the Class

Continue Read-Aloud

Book Preview Mini-Lesson

TUESDAY

Teacher/Librarian Book Chats

Buzz About Books

D.E.A.R.

Book Preview Mini-Lesson

WEDNESDAY

Continue Read-Aloud

Freewrite About Books

Check with a Few Students on Reading Goals

D.E.A.R.

Book Preview Mini-Lesson

THURSDAY

Continue Read-Aloud

Status of the Class

Check with a Few Students on Reading Goals

D.E.A.R.

Book Preview Mini-Lesson

FRIDAY

Update Reading Logs

D.E.A.R.

Book Preview Mini-Lesson

WEEK 5

MONDAY

Meet with Librarian to Select Target Student 2

Poetry Break (Chapter 8)
- Remember that kids can read aloud with a partner—with you, too!
- Have a special shelf or stack of poetry books within easy reach.
- Provide enough time for this—they may need five to eight minutes just to find a book.

Status of the Class

Continue Read-Aloud

Book Preview Mini-Lesson

TUESDAY

Teacher/Librarian Book Chats

Buzz About Books

D.E.A.R.

Book Preview Mini-Lesson

WEDNESDAY

Continue Read-Aloud

Freewrite About Books

Check with a Few Students on Reading Goals

D.E.A.R.

Book Preview Mini-Lesson

THURSDAY

Continue Read-Aloud

Status of the Class

Read Around

Book Preview Mini-Lesson

FRIDAY

Meet with Librarian and Target Student 2 (not during class time)

Update Reading Logs

D.E.A.R.

Book Preview Mini-Lesson

WEEK 6

MONDAY

Elementary or YA Café Meets (Chapter 8)

Status of the Class

Continue Read-Aloud

Book Preview Mini-Lesson

TUESDAY

Teacher/Librarian Book Chats

Buzz About Books

D.E.A.R.

Book Preview Mini-Lesson

WEDNESDAY

Continue Read-Aloud

Freewrite About Books

Check with a Few Students on Reading Goals

D.E.A.R.

Book Preview Mini-Lesson

THURSDAY

Continue Read-Aloud

Status of the Class

Picture Book of the Month Meeting (Chapter 8)
- Private lunch meeting with those who have read (K–5 students only).
- Extra credit point given to middle/high school students who have read.

D.E.A.R.

Book Preview Mini-Lesson

FRIDAY

Update Reading Logs

Read Aloud and Discuss the Picture Book of the Month (whole class) (Chapter 8)

Book Preview Mini-Lesson

WEEK 7

MONDAY

Teacher Tells a Personal Book Story (Chapter 5)

Introduce Picture Book of the Month

Status of the Class

Continue Read-Aloud

Book Preview Mini-Lesson

TUESDAY

Teacher/Librarian Book Chats

Buzz About Books

D.E.A.R.

Book Preview Mini-Lesson

WEDNESDAY

Continue Read-Aloud

Freewrite About Books

Check with a Few Students on Reading Goals

D.E.A.R.

Book Preview Mini-Lesson

THURSDAY

Continue Read-Aloud

Status of the Class

Check with a Few Students on Reading Goals

D.E.A.R.

Book Preview Mini-Lesson

FRIDAY

Update Reading Logs

Shopping Trip 2 in the Library

D.E.A.R.

Book Preview Mini-Lesson

WEEK 8

MONDAY

Comic Book Break (Chapter 8)

- Lots of comics need to be available! Again, garage sales. Ask staff in the district if they have comics to donate to you!

Status of the Class

Continue Read-Aloud

Book Preview Mini-Lesson

TUESDAY

Teacher/Librarian Book Chats

Buzz About Books

D.E.A.R.

Book Preview Mini-Lesson

WEDNESDAY

Continue Read-Aloud

Freewrite About Books

Check with a Few Students on Reading Goals

D.E.A.R.

Book Preview Mini-Lesson

THURSDAY

Continue Read-Aloud

Status of the Class

Check with a Few Students on Reading Goals

D.E.A.R.

Book Preview Mini-Lesson

FRIDAY

Update Reading Logs

D.E.A.R.

Book Preview Mini-Lesson

WEEK 9

MONDAY

Newspaper Day (Chapter 8)

Status of the Class

Meet with a Few Students to Assess Progress Toward Reading Goal for This Quarter

Continue Read-Aloud

Book Preview Mini-Lesson

TUESDAY

Teacher/Librarian Book Chats

Meet with a Few Students to Assess Progress Toward Reading Goal for This Quarter

Continue Read-Aloud

Buzz About Books

Book Preview Mini-Lesson

WEDNESDAY

Meet with a Few Students to Assess Progress Toward Reading Goal for This Quarter

Continue Read-Aloud

Freewrite About Books

Book Preview Mini-Lesson

THURSDAY

Meet with a Few Students to Assess Progress Toward Reading Goal for This Quarter

Continue Read-Aloud

Status of the Class

Book Preview Mini-Lesson

FRIDAY

Update Reading Logs

Complete and Discuss Read-Aloud 1

Highlight Other Titles by Read–Aloud Author (Chapter 4)
- Be sure the librarian knows in advance which authors you are reading aloud from each year and that she or he checks for any new titles to add to the library collection.
- Reserve titles a couple of weeks in advance so they can be available for your students to see on the day you complete your read-aloud.

YEAR END

Students Take Final Reading Survey (Chapter 2)
- They will compare this to the survey taken at the beginning of the year.
- Consider the reflective writing assignment I call a "changed reader paper" as well as the trade-the-grade option.
- Plan for this around Week 7 of the final quarter so there is ample time to complete it.

Until Next Time . . .

I opened Chapter 1 with the story of young Marie Boone, whose passion and confidence so inspired me during a school visit many years ago. It was a late evening in May 2009 when I finally spoke to Marie again. Six years had passed since we had first met at Woodrow Wilson School when she was in the fifth grade. Six years since she had asked me those big questions about going to college. Six years since I had mailed her a box of books.

I could scarcely wait for the update, and what I learned heartened me! Marie would be finishing up her high school career the next year. She still planned on going to college, and she was still a reader and a writer. She told me she had recently completed the Left Behind series by Tim LaHaye and Jerry Jenkins. She then recounted that many of her teachers over the years had remarked on how high her scores were on reading and writing tests—and that those same teachers had encouraged her to move forward and allow her skills to blossom. She has apparently taken their advice.

Marie remembered my visit from all those year ago. She told me, on this May evening, that her mind had been racing with questions as I visited with the boys and girls of Woodrow Wilson School that day and that it had been a significant moment in her life when she was allowed to stay behind after the presentation and ask her questions. She also remembered the box of books and the letter I had mailed to her. She told me that she still had them, and I hope that is true.

My heartfelt prayer for teachers everywhere is that you will all take that extra step—that you'll go out of your way, above and beyond, to ignite a passion for reading in your students. The teacher's manuals aren't going to tell you to do it and neither is the district curriculum guide (unless I helped write it). I'm hoping you'll just do it because you know it's the right thing to do and because it's what needs to be done—for the Marie Boones of this world . . . and for all of the others. And, I really hope my book will help.

Take care. Call someone who's not expecting to hear from you. Go last when you could be first. Handwrite your thank-you notes. Teach the children—and treat them well.

Keeping the Literacy Lamp Burning,

Steven L. Layne

APPENDIX A

Resources for Locating the Best Children's/YA Books

Publishers Weekly has a fall and spring edition focused exclusively on the children's market, which provides the latest information on new books at every grade level. It is possible to subscribe to only these two editions of *PW* if you are a member of the Society of Children's Book Writers and Illustrators (SCBWI). You can also call 1-800-278-2991 to inquire about purchasing these single issues. Visit www.publishersweekly.com and select Children's Books or Children's Authors on their "browse topics" search option for tremendous information.

Each year, the October issue of *The Reading Teacher* publishes the list of "Children's Choices." This award listing of books is sponsored jointly by the International Reading Association and the Children's Book Council. The list contains the top 100 new titles for children ages five through thirteen as selected by 10,000 children from across the United States. Each title is annotated. Contact IRA at 1-800-336-7323 or visit the Web site at http://www.reading.org/Resources/Booklists/ChildrensChoices.aspx.

Each year, the November issue of *The Reading Teacher* publishes the list of "Teachers' Choices." This award listing of books is sponsored by the International Reading Association. The list contains thirty new titles for children ages five to fourteen as selected by teachers, reading specialists, and librarians from different regions across the United States. Each title is annotated. Contact IRA at 1-800-336-7323 or visit the Web site at http://www.reading.org/Resources/Booklists/TeachersChoices.aspx.

Each year, the November issue of *The Journal of Adolescent and Adult Literacy* publishes the list of "Young Adults' Choices." This award listing of books is sponsored by the International Reading Association. The list contains thirty new titles for young adults in grades seven through twelve as selected by 4,500 of their peers from different regions across the United States. Each title is annotated. Contact IRA at 1-800-336-7323 or visit the Web site at http://www.reading.org/Resources/Booklists/YoungAdultsChoices.aspx.

Booklinks is a wonderful quarterly supplement included with a subscription to Booklist—an imprint of the American Library Association. *Booklinks* features wonderful themed book annotations at a wide range of reading levels. It's a classroom teacher's dream for connecting books with the curriculum. Examples of themes include: Setting the West 1800–1900, Sharing the Passion of Science, and A Look at Alphabet Books of the '90s. *Booklist* releases reviews of newly published books in the domain of children's and young adult literature, as well as providing wonderful feature articles of interest to teachers and librarians.

A wonderful resource for those working with young adults is *Voice of Youth Advocates (VOYA).* This magazine is published April through February on a bimonthly basis and contains excellent articles and resources for those interested in young adult literature. Send questions or requests for information to voya@voya.com or phone 1-800-233-1687 for subscription information. Visit the Web site at www.voya.com.

The Journal of Children's Literature is published twice annually by the Children's Literature Assembly—a special-interest group of the National Council of Teachers of English. Contact NCTE for information at 1-877-369-6283 or visit their Web site at www.ncte.org. An Internet search for this journal by title is the quickest way to subscribe or to receive more information.

The Dragon Lode is a journal of the Children's Literature and Reading Special Interest Group of the International Reading Association. This journal is published twice annually. Contact IRA for more information at 1-800-336-7323 or visit their Web site at www.reading.org. An Internet search for this journal by title is the quickest way to subscribe or to receive more information.

The ALAN Review is published three times annually by the Assembly on Literature for Adolescents Network—a special-interest group of the National Council of Teachers of English. Contact NCTE for information at 1-877-369-6283 or visit their Web site at www.ncte.org. An Internet search for this journal by title is the quickest way to subscribe or to receive more information.

SIGNAL is a journal of the Special Interest Group—Network on Literature for Adolescents
   of the International Reading Association. This journal is published twice annually. Contact
   IRA for more information at 1-800-336-7323 or visit their Web site at www.reading.org. An
   Internet search for this journal by title is the quickest way to subscribe or to receive more
   information.

More Resources for Locating the Best Children's Books

Please be aware that all of the URLs listed here were functioning at the time this
appendix was prepared. Changes can and do occur on a regular basis.

www.ala.org/alsc/caldecott.html

www.ala.org/alsc/newbery.html

www.bookadventure.org

www.bookmuse.com

www.childrenslit.com

www.guysread.com

www.peggysharp.com

www.cynthialeitichsmith.com

APPENDIX B

Fifteen Great Magazines for Kids

Cicada: Age range: 6–9. Literary focus.

Cobblestone: Age range: 8–14. Focus is American history.

Creative Kids: Age range: 8–14. Focus is stories, games, and puzzles written by and for kids.

Highlights for Children: Age range: 2–12. General interest.

Ladybug: Age range: 2–6. General interest for young children.

Merlyn's Pen: Age range: 11–16. Focus is stories, poems, and expository pieces written by teens.

National Geographic World: Age range: 8–14. Focus is natural history, science, and outdoors.

Owl: The Discovery Magazine for Kids: Age range: 8–13. Focus is nature, science, and technology.

Ranger Rick: Age range: 6–12. Focus is animals and nature.

Skipping Stones: Age range: 8–18. Focus is multicultural stories for and by kids.

Spider: Age range: 6–9. General interest.

Sports Illustrated for Kids: Age range: 8–14. Focus is professional and amateur sports.

Stone Soup: Age range: 6–14. Focus is stories, poems, and expository pieces written by kids.

Time for Kids: Age range: 9–12. Weekly news magazine. General interest.

U*S* Kids: Age range: 6–11. Historical focus with stories, games, puzzles, and interactive activities.

APPENDIX C

Picture Book of the Month
SUGGESTED TITLES FOR PICTURE BOOK OF THE MONTH, GRADES K–2

One Dog Canoe	Mary Casanova
Raccoon Tune	Nancy Shaw
Miss Smith's Incredible Storybook	Michael Garland
Ten Puppies	Lynn Reiser
My Little Sister Ate One Hare	Bill Grossman
Boo to a Goose	Mem Fox
Carlo Likes Reading	Jessica Spanyol
Love the Baby	Steven L. Layne
Where's My Teddy?	Jez Alborough
Score One for the Sloths	Helen Lester
The Two Terrible Frights	Jim Aylesworth
The War Between the Vowels and the Consonants	Priscilla Turner
Beverly Billingsly Borrows a Book	Alexander Stadler
I Love My Little Storybook	Anita Jeram
Q Is for Duck	Mary Elting and Michael Folsom
Old Black Fly	Jim Aylesworth
No Matter What	Debi Gliori
First Day Jitters	Julie Danneberg
Lily's Purple Plastic Purse	Kevin Henkes
A Fine, Fine School	Sharon Creech
Mud Is Cake	Pam Muñoz Ryan
It's Okay to Be Different	Todd Parr

PICTURE BOOK OF THE MONTH: SCHOOL THEMES

August	*First Day Jitters*	Julie Danneberg
September	*T Is for Teachers: A School Alphabet*	Steven L. Layne and Deborah Dover Layne
October	*Teachers' Night Before Halloween*	Steven L. Layne
November	*Miss Nelson Is Missing*	Harry G. Allard Jr.
December	*The Teachers' Night Before Christmas*	Steven L. Layne
January	*Miss Malarkey Won't Be in Today*	Judy Finchler
February	*If You Take a Mouse to School*	Laura Numeroff
March	*Number 1 Teacher: A School Counting Book*	Steven L. Layne
April	*A Fine, Fine School*	Sharon Creech
May	*Thank You, Mr. Falker*	Patricia Polacco

SUGGESTED TITLES FOR PICTURE BOOK OF THE MONTH, GRADES 3–8

Dear Mrs. LaRue: Letters from Obedience School	Mark Teague
The Secret Knowledge of Grown-Ups	David Wisniewski
Fireboat: The Heroic Adventures of the John J. Harvey	Maira Kalman
My Brother Dan's Delicious	Steven L. Layne
A Story for Bear	Dennis Haseley
The Other Side	Jacqueline Woodson
Zathura	Chris Van Allsburg
If You Hopped Like a Frog	David M. Schwartz
David Gets in Trouble	David Shannon
Miss Alaineus: A Vocabulary Disaster	Debra Frasier
The Wolf Who Cried Boy	Bob Hartman
Miss Malarkey Won't Be in Today	Judy Finchler

The True Story of the Three Little Pigs	Jon Scieszka
A Fine, Fine School	Sharon Creech
The Bat Boy and His Violin	Gavin Curtis
The Mysteries of Harris Burdick	Chris Van Allsburg
The Teachers' Night Before Christmas	Steven L. Layne
Mailing May	Michael O. Tunnell
Shrek!	William Steig
Who Says a Dog Goes Bow-Wow?	Hank De Zutter
Testing Miss Malarkey	Judy Finchler
How Much Is a Million?	David M. Schwartz
The Three Little Dinosaurs	Jim Harris
A Grain of Rice	Helena Clare Pittman
The Widow's Broom	Chris Van Allsburg
The Bravest Ever Bear	Allan Ahlberg
Thomas's Sheep and the Great Geography Test	Steven L. Layne
Beware of Boys	Tony Blundell
Serendipity	Tobi Tobias

APPENDIX D

FILLABLE FORMS

What Do You Like? Inventory

Name _____

Put an "X" by the things you like.

_____ animals	_____ trains
_____ tools	_____ circus
_____ dancing	_____ jokes
_____ books	_____ bugs
_____ sports	_____ cooking
_____ games	_____ computers
_____ music	_____ art

Reading and Me Inventory

 ## Reading and Me

Name _____

1. How well do you think you read?

   ☺   😐   ☹

2. How do you feel about reading at home?

   ☺   😐   ☹

3. How do you feel about reading at school?

   ☺   😐   ☹

4. Do you have books at home that you read?

             Yes   No

5. What are your favorite TV shows? _____

_____.

6. What is the best movie(s) you have seen? _____

_____.

7. If an author could write a book just for you, what would it be about?

_____

_____

_____.

Reading and Me Inventory

Circle what you like to read:

comic books	magazines	newspapers
nonfiction books	poetry	plays
mysteries	funny books	adventure books
"how to" books	books about the past	

Circle what you like to read about or what you want to learn more about:

famous people	music	other countries
insects	dancing	sports
aliens	monsters	jokes
poetry	solar system	friends
animals	planes	cars
cooking	making crafts	drawing

Other _____

_____

_____

_____

_____ .

T. Tuttle, 2009

Interest Inventory

Name _____

Place a check beside anything on the list below that you would like to know more about.

____ auto mechanics	____ construction	____ electronics
____ famous people	____ woodwork	____ history
____ motion pictures	____ foreign lands	____ printing
____ electricity	____ art	____ circus
____ music	____ monsters	____ poetry
____ theater	____ computers	____ animals
____ insects	____ science	____ cars
____ dancing	____ singers	____ planes
____ geography	____ detectives	____ outer space
____ cooking	____ jokes	____ radio
____ sports	____ writing	____ trains

If an author wrote a book just for you, what would it be about? _____

_____.

If _____ recommended a book for me, I would probably read it.

Circle what you like to read.

comic books	animal stories	magazines	science fiction
mysteries	humorous books	newspapers	historical fiction
romances	biographies	plays	adventure stories
poetry	short stories	fantasies	"how to" books

Interest Inventory   Name _____

1. What do you like to do in your spare time?

2. Do you belong to any clubs or organizations? If so, what are they?

3. What kinds of movies do you like?

4. Do you have any favorite sports?

5. If you had three wishes, what would they be?

6. What kind of books do you own?

7. If you had a surprise day off from school, how would you spend it?

8. If you could transport yourself to any time or place in the past, where would you go?

9. If you had the chance to meet any famous person, living or dead, who would it be?

10. If you could pick any three books from a bookstore for free, what might they be about?

11. If you could go on a trip to any place in the world today, where would you go?

Initial Self-Assessment—Reading

Name _____

1. I enjoy reading the following types of print:

   ☐ books ☐ magazines ☐ newspapers

   ☐ poems ☐ short stories ☐ plays

2. I choose to read books that are not assigned in school . . .

   ☐ often ☐ sometimes ☐ never

3. My attitude about reading is . . .

   ☐ positive ☐ neutral ☐ negative

4. I like to read books from the following genres:

   ☐ nonfiction—informational ☐ historical fiction ☐ science fiction

   ☐ traditional fantasy ☐ modern fantasy—low ☐ modern fantasy— high

   ☐ nonfiction—biography ☐ nonfiction—autobiography ☐ realistic fiction—mystery

   ☐ realistic fiction—adventure ☐ realistic fiction—humor ☐ realistic fiction—classics

5. When I compare books that I have really enjoyed, some things they all have in common are _____
   _____ .

6. The best book I've ever read is _____
   _____ .

7. Some of my favorite authors are _____
   _____.

8. I could improve my reading skills if _____
   _____.

9. People whose book recommendations I value include _____
   _____.

10. I could make more time for recreational reading if _____
   _____.

11. A reading goal that I would like to achieve for this school year is _____
   _____.

Final Self-Assessment—Reading

Name _____

1. I enjoy reading the following types of print:

   ☐ books   ☐ magazines   ☐ newspapers

   ☐ poems   ☐ short stories   ☐ plays

2. I choose to read books that are not assigned in school . . .

   ☐ often   ☐ sometimes   ☐ never

3. My attitude about reading is . . .

   ☐ positive   ☐ neutral   ☐ negative

4. I like to read books from the following genres:

   ☐ nonfiction—informational   ☐ historical fiction   ☐ science fiction

   ☐ traditional fantasy   ☐ modern fantasy—low   ☐ modern fantasy—high

   ☐ nonfiction—biography   ☐ nonfiction—autobiography   ☐ realistic fiction—mystery

   ☐ realistic fiction—adventure ☐ realistic fiction—humor   ☐ realistic fiction classics

5. I have grown this year as a reader because _____

   _____ .

6. The reading selection that I liked the most this year was titled _____

   _____ .

7. I liked this selection because _____

   _____ .

8. The reading selection that I liked the least this year was titled _____

   _____ .

9. I did not enjoy this selection because _____

   _____ .

10. A book I enjoyed that was recommended to me this year was titled _____

    _____

    _____ .

11. Some of my favorite authors are _____

    _____

    _____ .

Final Self-Assessment—Reading (cont.)

Name _____

12.　This year, my reading skills have . . .

☐ improved a lot　　　☐ improved a little　　　☐ stayed the same

13.　This year my recreational reading habits have . . .

☐ improved　　　☐ stayed the same　　　☐ declined

People whose book recommendations I value include _____

_____

_____

_____.

A reading goal that I would like to achieve for next school year is _____

_____

_____

_____.

Reading Goal Sheet

Name _____

Reading Goal for _____ Quarter

- • A strong reading goal will
- • Stretch you in some new way
- • Motivate and interest you
- • Be reasonable

My goal this quarter is _____

_____

_____

_____

_____

_____.

This is a strong goal for me because _____

_____

_____

_____

_____.

Book Chat Preparation Sheet

BOOK CHAT # _____   **GRADE LEVELS** _____

TITLE: _____

AUTHOR: _____**PUB. DATE:** _____

PUBLISHER: _____ **ISBN:** _____

HOOK: _____

_____

_____

_____

_____

_____

_____.

NOTES: _____

_____

_____

_____

_____

_____.

OTHER BOOKS BY AUTHOR: _____

_____

_____

_____.

Reading Log Selections

Name _____ Grade _____

Qtr	Title	Author	Genre	Rating

Someday Book List

Name _____

Title   Author

_____

_____

_____

_____

_____

_____

_____

_____

_____

_____

_____

_____

_____

_____

_____

_____

_____

Books to Consider

From Shopping: _____

_____

_____

_____

_____

_____

From Book Chats: _____

_____

_____

_____

_____

From Recommendations: _____

_____

_____

_____

_____

From Read Arounds: _____

_____

_____

_____

_____

Book Chat Evaluation Rubric

Student's Name _____   Comments

EFFECTIVE HOOK/INTRODUCTION   _____ /04

- ☐ creative, attention-getter (2)
- ☐ author and title identified
- ☐ genre correctly identified

BOOK CLEARLY SHOWN TO AUDIENCE   _____ /02

MAIN CHARACTER(S) INTRODUCED   _____ /12
(LIMIT: THREE)

- ☐ protagonist/antagonist (as applicable)
- ☐ age
- ☐ physical description
- ☐ personality (general disposition, chief likes/dislikes)
- ☐ primary goal(s) of character
- ☐ comparison drawn to a well-known character or real-life person

SUPPORTING CHARACTERS INTRODUCED   _____ /03
(LIMIT: FOUR)

- ☐ relationship to main character
- ☐ role in story
- ☐ additional pertinent information as needed

PLOT DISCUSSED PRECISELY   _____ /14
AND CONCISELY

- ☐ setting(s)
- ☐ major problem
- ☐ complications
- ☐ climax
- ☐ resolution
- ☐ conflict(s)
- ☐ theme(s)

[Discussion of the plot should move in the order presented here: setting, major problem, complications, climax, etc. Each of these words must be *specifically* stated aloud during the Book Chat. These words must also be in boldface type in the manuscript.]

Book Chat Evaluation Rubric (cont.)

POWERFUL PASSAGE READ-ALOUD _____ /07

☐ sufficient background provided

☐ passage is dramatic/climactic

☐ superior oral reading (3)

DELIVERY _____ /12

☐ volume

☐ rate

☐ enunciation/articulation

☐ pitch/tone

☐ eye contact

☐ stage presence

CLOSING _____ /03

☐ creative (2)

☐ clear closure

MANUSCRIPT _____ /19

☐ strong vocabulary (3)

☐ clear transitions (3)

☐ bold headings with reduced type size as per model (2)

☐ cohesive written text (4)

☐ strong writing mechanics (4)

☐ **APPEARANCE OF MANUSCRIPT (3)**

OVERALL IMPRESSION _____ /20

TIME ALLOCATION MET (8 MIN. MAX) _____ /04

TOTAL _____ /100

GRADE _____

Delivery Start Time _____ : _____

Delivery Stop Time _____ : _____

First Read Club Sticker

This book was
First Read by:

_____

BOOKS BY STEVEN L. LAYNE

Layne, S. L. 2011. *Paradise Lost*. Gretna, LA: Pelican.

Layne, S. L., and D. D. Layne. 2010. *W Is for Windy City: A Chicago Alphabet*. Chelsea, MI: Sleeping Bear.

Layne, S. L. 2009. *Igniting a Passion for Reading: Successful Strategies for Building Lifetime Readers*. Portland, ME: Stenhouse.

Layne, S. L. 2008. *Teachers' Night Before Halloween*. Gretna, LA: Pelican.

Layne, S. L., and D. D. Layne. 2008. *Number 1 Teacher: A School Counting Book*. Chelsea, MI: Sleeping Bear.

Layne, S. L. 2007. *Love the Baby*. Gretna, LA: Pelican.

Layne, S. L. 2006. *Mergers*. Gretna, LA: Pelican.

Layne, S. L. 2005. *Verses for Mom's Heart*. Gretna, LA: Pelican.

Layne, S. L., and D. D. Layne. 2005. *T Is for Teachers: A School Alphabet*. Chelsea, MI: Sleeping Bear.

Layne, S. L. 2005. *Over Land and Sea: A Story of International Adoption*. Gretna, LA: Pelican.

Layne, S. L. 2004. *Verses for Dad's Heart*. Gretna, LA: Pelican.

Layne, S. L. 2004. *The Principal's Night Before Christmas*. Gretna, LA: Pelican.

Layne, S. L. 2004. *Thomas's Sheep and the Spectacular Science Project*. Gretna, LA: Pelican.

Layne, S. L. 2003. *My Brother Dan's Delicious*. Gretna, LA: Pelican.

Layne, S. L. 2002. *This Side of Paradise*. Gretna, LA: Pelican.

Layne, S. L. 2001. *Life's Literacy Lessons: Poems for Teachers*. Newark, DE: International Reading Association.

Layne, S. L. 2001. *The Teachers' Night Before Christmas*. Gretna, LA: Pelican.

Layne, S. L. 1998. *Thomas's Sheep and the Great Geography Test*. Gretna, LA: Pelican.

BIBLIOGRAPHY

Anderson, R. C., E. H. Hiebert, J. A. Scott, and I. A. G. Wilkinson. 1985. *Becoming a Nation of Readers: The Report of the Commission on Reading.* Washington, DC: U.S. Department of Education.

Boorstin, D. 1984. *Books in Our Future: A Report from the Librarian of Congress to the Congress.* Washington, DC: Library of Congress.

The Conference Board, Corporate Voices for Working Families, the Partnership for 21st Century Skills, and the Society for Human Resource Management. 2006. *Are They Really Ready to Work? Employers' Perspectives on the Basic Knowledge and Applied Skills of New Entrants to the 21st Century U.S. Workforce.* New York: The Conference Board. Available online at http://www.21stcenturyskills.org/documents/FINAL_REPORT_PDF09-29-06.pdf.

Gallagher, K. 2009. *Readicide: How Schools Are Killing Reading and What You Can Do About It.* Portland, ME: Stenhouse.

Hahn, M. L. 2002. *Reconsidering Read-Aloud.* Portland, ME: Stenhouse.

Hoffman, J. V., N. L. Roser, and J. Battle. 1993. "Reading Aloud in Classrooms: From the Modal Toward a 'Model.'" The Reading Teacher 46: 496–503.

Kaiser Family Foundation. 2003. *Zero to Six: Electronic Media in the Lives of Infants, Toddlers, and Preschoolers.* Available online at http://www.kff.org/entmedia/upload/Zero-to-Six-Electronic-Media-in-the-Lives-of-Infants-Toddlers-and-Preschoolers-PDF.pdf.

Layne, Steven L. 2001. *Life's Literacy Lessons: Poems for Teachers.* Newark, DE: International Reading Association.

Lesesne, Teri. 2003. *Making the Match: The Right Book for the Right Reader at the Right Time, Grades 4–12.* Portland, ME: Stenhouse.

Mayne, E. 1915. "The Object of Teaching Reading." In *Methods, Aids, and Devices for Teachers,* ed. W. J. Beecher and G. B. Faxon. Dansville, NY: FA Owen.

Mikulecky, L. 1979. "A Changing View of Literacy." *Reporting on Reading* 5 (3): 1–5.

National Center for Education Statistics. 1997. *Digest of Education Statistics*. Washington, DC: U.S. Department of Education.

———. 2008. *National Assessment of Educational Progress*. Washington, DC: U.S. Department of Education.

National Endowment for the Arts. 2007. *To Read or Not to Read: A Question of National Consequence*. Washington, DC: National Endowment for the Arts. Available online at http://www.nea.gov/research/ToRead.PDF.

National Institute of Child Health and Human Development. 2000. *Report of the National Reading Panel. Teaching Children to Read: An Evidence-Based Assessment of the Scientific Research Literature on Reading and Its Implications for Reading Instruction* (NIH Publication No. 00-4769). Washington, DC: U.S. Government Printing Office.

Trelease, J. 2006/2007. *The Read-Aloud Handbook*. 6th ed. New York: Penguin.

Tunnell, M. O., and J. S. Jacobs. 2008. *Children's Literature, Briefly*. 4th ed. Upper Saddle River, NJ: Pearson/Prentice Hall.

Weeks, L. 2001. "The No-Book Report: Skim It and Weep." *Washington Post*, May 14. Available online at http://www.washingtonpost.com/ac2/wp-dyn/A23370-2001May13?language=printer.

Children's and Young Adult Books

Alexander, Lloyd. 1999. *The Book of Three*. New York: Macmillan.

Alphin, Elaine Marie. 2000. *Counterfeit Son*. New York: Houghton Mifflin Harcourt.

Avi. 1990. *The True Confessions of Charlotte Doyle*. New York: Scholastic.

Brashares, Ann. 2004. *The Sisterhood of the Traveling Pants*. New York: Dell.

Brennan-Nelson, Denise. 2005. *Someday Is Not a Day of the Week*. Chelsea, MI: Sleeping Bear.

Carter, Ally. 2006. *I'd Tell You I Love You, but Then I'd Have to Kill You*. New York: Hyperion.

Christie, Agatha. 1944. *And Then There Were None*. New York: Pocket Books.

Cleary, Beverly. 1965. *The Mouse and the Motorcycle*. New York: HarperCollins.

Collier, James Lincoln, and Christopher Collier. 1985. *My Brother Sam Is Dead*. New York: Scholastic.

Crisp, Marty. 2000. *My Dog, Cat*. New York: Holiday House.

Dowell, Frances O'Roark. 2001. *Dovey Coe*. New York: Aladdin.

Fox, Mem. 1994. *Tough Boris*. New York: Houghton Mifflin Harcourt.

Haddix, Margaret Peterson. 2002. *Among the Hidden*. New York: Simon and Schuster.

Henkes, Kevin. 1996. *Lily's Purple Plastic Purse*. New York: HarperCollins.

Layne, Steven L. 2001. *This Side of Paradise*. Nampa, ID: North Star Books.

L'Engle, Madeleine. 1962. *A Wrinkle in Time*. New York: Dell.

Lewis, C. S. 1978. *The Lion, the Witch, and the Wardrobe*. New York: HarperCollins.

Lowry, Lois. 1989. *Number the Stars*. New York: Houghton Mifflin Harcourt.

———. 1993. *The Giver*. New York: Houghton Mifflin Harcourt.

O'Connor, Jane. 2005. *Fancy Nancy*. New York: HarperCollins.

Paulsen, Gary. 1998. *The Transall Saga*. New York: Delacorte.

Pennypacker, Sara. 2006. *Clementine*. New York: Hyperion.

Raskin, Ellen. 1978. *The Westing Game*. London: Puffin Books.

Roberts, Willo Davis. 1998. *The Kidnappers: A Mystery*. New York: Atheneum.

Shusterman, Neal. 2003. *Full Tilt*. New York: Simon and Schuster.

———. 2007. *Unwind*. New York: Simon and Schuster.

Werlin, Nancy. 2008. *The Rules of Survival*. New York: Penguin.